To Nancy — who lives the
Path of Blessing. Love,
Sandi

THE
PATH
OF
BLESSING

THE
PATH
OF
BLESSING

Experiencing
the Energy and Abundance
of the Divine

Marcia Prager

Bell Tower ⬛ New York

Grateful acknowledgment is made to the following for permission to
reprint previously published material:
Lyric excerpts of "Shall I Tell You What I Think of You" by Richard Rodgers
and Oscar Hammerstein II. Copyright © 1951 by Richard Rodgers and Oscar
Hammerstein II. Copyright renewed. Williamson Music owner of publication
and allied rights throughout the world. International copyright secured.
Reprinted by permission. All rights reserved.
The poems on pages 89 and 168 are translated by Jonathan Star and
Shahram Shiva from the book, *A Garden Beyond Paradise: the Mystical Poetry of Rumi.*
Excerpts from *Meditations with Meister Eckhart,* edited by Matthew Fox.
Copyright © 1983 by Bear & Co., Santa Fe, NM.

Published by Bell Tower, an imprint of Harmony Books,
a division of Crown Publishers, Inc.,
201 East 50th Street, New York, New York 10022.
Member of the Crown Publishing Group.

Random House, Inc. New York, Toronto, London, Sydney, Auckland
www.randomhouse.com

Bell Tower and colophon are trademarks of Crown Publishers, Inc.
Printed in the United States of America
Design by Meryl Sussman Levavi/Digitext, Inc.

Library of Congress Cataloging-in-Publication Data
Prager, Marcia.
The path of blessing: experiencing the energy and abundance of
the divine / Marcia Prager.—1st ed.
includes bibliographical references.
1. Benedictions. 2. Barukh atah adonai elohenu melekh ha'olam
(the Hebrew phrase) 3. Spiritual life—Judaism. I. Title.
BM675.B4z836 1998
296.4'5—DC21   98-2903
                                                          CIP

ISBN 0-517-70363-7
2 4 6 8 10 9 7 5 3

Contents

❦

v

Words of Praise

☙✲❧

In times past, rabbis were traditionally called upon to give their imprimatur to new works of sacred teaching. While this is no longer the custom, I would like to set such an imprimatur on Rabbi Marcia's work. This is to emphasize that you are not merely reading a book but studying Torah, and that her work is another link in the chain of our sacred tradition. In such imprimaturs the following phrase was often used: "In owning this book, you will bring blessing into your home." Rabbi Marcia's book deserves an honored place close to where you pray and meditate.

How much I wish that earlier voice-givers for the *Shekhinah* had written down their sacred teachings. If Channah Rochel of Ludmir had left us her writings, how blessed we would be at this time when women are beginning to take their rightful place as teachers of Torah.

Done this second day of the week of *Lekh Lekha*, in which God promises our ancestor: "And you shall be a blessing," 5758.

Rabbi Zalman Schachter-Shalomi

Rabbi Zalman Schachter-Shalomi

Preface and Acknowledgments

☙❀❧

The seeds of this work began to germinate while I was still a rabbinical student endeavoring to teach a few private students elementary Hebrew and the basic structure of Hebrew prayer. Hebrew is such a rich spiritual language. It has a glow and depth that few translations can ever capture. Words sparkle with inner meanings and dance with inner light like jewels in a treasure chest. Yet for those of us who were not raised with Hebrew, that treasure chest is hard to open. For my students, mastering Hebrew just to learn or pray felt like a daunting prerequisite, but they so longed to find their way in.

I myself recall when, having left an academic life at a major secular university to enter rabbinical study, I was invited by Rabbi Zalman Schachter-Shalomi to see him at home during one of my first weeks in Philadelphia. It was the beginning of a special relationship for me. But what I most remember about the visit was his library.

My life has revolved around universities since my undergraduate days, and I can find my way comfortably around almost any major library. Here in Reb Zalman's library I was silenced. Two large rooms of floor-to-ceiling bookcases bulged with books everywhere, on tables, desks, and hassocks. It was a library from another world, crammed with aging brown-leather volumes whose tarnished gold stamping announced titles I'd never heard of. I ran my hand over the bindings. This was a library of the spiritual wisdom of my people, and I had no idea what it contained. I could not name one author, could barely read a word, I for whom Harvard's Widener Library was a breeze.

Over the ensuing years, under Reb Zalman's guidance, and with the help of teachers like Rabbi Arthur Green and Rabbi Miles Krassen, the world of these texts began to open up for me. I can read them better now, and much of whatever wisdom this book contains comes from them.

But what should I say to those who came to *me* to learn? Few of us can take years to learn to read Hebrew, much less the insider language of Hasidic authors. While many of these works have been translated during the fifteen years since my first visit to Reb Zalman's study, Hebrew still remains a vital gateway to Jewish learning and Jewish prayer.

I began to see, however, that (while I would never discourage it) to enter the world of Jewish prayer, one need not be fluent in modern Hebrew at all. In fact, as I *steeped* myself more and more deeply in the practice of Hebrew prayer, it became clear that a vocabulary as small as a hundred words, well taught, would open up a vast panorama of Jewish spiritual wisdom. I decided to teach "hundred-word" courses. But how to begin? Where should I start the hundred words? The answer was obvious. I should begin with the words of a blessing. Blessing is the foundation of Jewish prayer. My hundred-word course soon became a six-word course, as I began to explore the depths of meaning that lay in each of the six opening words of a Hebrew blessing. When Howard Lesnick suggested doing a book, it was these six words of blessing my heart raced to.

❧

Many extraordinary people participated in the birthing of this work, most especially my friends and students who came to join me in exploring the inner dimension of the Hebrew letters and words of prayer and blessing. I am grateful to the Philadelphia P'nai Or Religious Fellowship congregation, which has been a fertile greenhouse for new forms of experiential learning and prayer. The Jewish Renewal Life Center, founded by Rabbi Julie Greenberg, has afforded me fourteen extraordinary semesters of teaching Jewish spirituality to sophisticated and dedicated seekers of Jewish soul-wisdom. At Elat Chayyim, the magnificent Jewish Renewal retreat center founded by Rabbis Jeff Roth and Joanna Katz, I have been able to teach each summer for the past five years. Both at Elat Chayyim and at the New York Open Center, I have taught "The Path of Blessing," and greatly deepened my own understanding of the power of this spiritual practice.

I would like again to thank my Rebbe, Reb Zalman, for his teaching, love, and support through all these years since we first met. The opportunity that I had to study under him during his years in Philadelphia has shaped my work and my life. My teachers, Rabbis Arthur Green and Miles Krassen, shared their own inner light with me and illuminated a way. Howard Lesnick, who had the vision that this teaching could become a book, labored to translate the stream-of-consciousness style of a charismatic oral teacher into a coherent manuscript, and edited the many versions more times than can be counted. He is a friend and colleague of the highest order.

Jeffrey and Shira Reiss backed this project with their support, and encouraged me to go forward when I despaired of ever achieving adequate eloquence to convey these teachings in print. Martha Trachtenberg, friend and professional editor, read the manuscript twice and contributed invaluable suggestions. I am also grateful to Rabbi Daniel Siegel, Maggid Yitzhok Buxbaum, and poet/author Rodger Kamenetz for their deep and insightful readings. Lynnel Jones worked sentence by sentence through the manuscript to nudge the writing toward a more fluid style. My student Barbara S. Sussman read each draft of the manuscript and joined her labor with mine to ensure the accuracy of the many pages of endnotes. Rabbi David Pearson's flair for detail and loving, constructive critiques enormously aided the task of completing the manuscript. I am deeply grateful for his scholarship and generosity of spirit. In the concluding phase of this work, thanks go to Susan Heckler of the New York Open Center and *Lapis* magazine, whose graceful commentary encouraged eleventh-hour revisions that opened up dense passages and brought greater clarity to the work as a whole. And I am especially grateful to Toinette Lippe, editorial director of Bell Tower, whose unceasing confidence that this work could make it to print kept the creative fires burning.

Naturally this work could not have happened without the support of my beloved husband and creative partner, *Hazzan* Jack Kessler. I would like to dedicate this book to him and to my beautiful eight-year-old son Aaron Reuven, who at age six, when I tucked him in at bedtime one night, sang the *Shema* with me and then looked up with his wondrous brown eyes and said: "Mommy,

when you breathe, you're talking to God, aren't you, Mommy?"
"Yes," I said, and together we took a long, deep breath.

With Heaven's aid, 7 Heshvan 5758, *Parashat Lekh Lekha*,
November 7, 1997

Author's Note

Throughout this work I have used gender-neutral language wherever possible. Translations and quotes that appear throughout the text may be altered very slightly to achieve that end. Translations from Hebrew texts are my own, taken from the original sources, unless otherwise indicated. Each chapter's endnotes will guide you to those and other sources, offering additional detail, explanation, and guidance for further exploration.

Meet Rabbi Marcia

એન્જ્ર

I first met Rabbi Marcia Prager in the fall of 1989. When Carolyn Schodt and I were married in 1976, we were both estranged from the faiths in which we had been raised. After a relatively conventional participation in Catholic and Jewish practices as adolescents, Carolyn and I had each found ourselves as young adults no longer able to continue that participation, although we acknowledged in our marriage ceremony the positive imprint that our differing religious legacies brought to our marriage.

During the next dozen years, we came increasingly to recognize and acknowledge our spiritual needs, through our deepening connection with the Quakers and annual summer visits with our children to a Buddhist community in California. By 1989, Carolyn had once more become willing to attend Mass, while I had several times tried to return to Jewish services, only to be reminded once again of the reasons I had left. Seeking a way to bring Jewish consciousness into our home, we stumbled, almost by accident, across Rabbi Marcia. It is no exaggeration to say that she has changed our lives, and yet that is not quite right: She has helped us to change our lives.

For the next year, we met in Marcia's study every ten days or so for an hour or more. We used the holidays of the Jewish calendar as the focus for an exploration of a Judaism that was almost as unknown to me as it was to Carolyn—a Judaism at once ancient and unfolding; grounded in the wisdom of centuries of Jewish sages and teachers, yet responsive to the wisdom of the modern and the postmodern world, and of other faith-traditions as well; respectful, even reverential, in its approach to Orthodoxy, yet always seeking and always finding in the stories and practices of that tradition, layers of meaning which underlie and give life to what has often seemed arid, at times even unpalatable.

Marcia often teaches in the Quaker community, among people of diverse religious backgrounds. She reports being able to tell who in the room were raised Jewish by observing them crying quietly as she describes a Judaism they never knew. "Why wasn't I taught this growing up?" many have asked her afterwards, plaintively or angrily.

Rabbi Marcia is a teacher, a preacher, a presence no less than a set of ideas. To reduce her to the printed page is a daring act. Yet it seemed to me important that what she has to offer go beyond those relatively few people who attend her services, study with her, or hear her speak. A few years ago, I suggested that we sit for a while with a tape recorder and talk, much as she had done with Carolyn and me earlier. She chose to focus on the familiar opening words of the traditional Hebrew blessing (brakha), ten words which embody the depth of Jewish spirituality. I had the tapes transcribed, and edited them, seeking to preserve the tone of one person speaking to another face-to-face. When Toinette Lippe, editorial director of Bell Tower, saw the power of Marcia Prager's teaching, and offered to work with her, Marcia began the hard work of converting this material into a book. We are grateful to Toinette for her vision and faith, and for her skills as an editor.

By now, I have worked on many drafts of this book. Each time there are passages that come to me as if for the first time, some that bring tears to my eyes or new light to my understanding. Each time my teacher's voice rises from the cold page like a song. Hear through her the voices and the spirit of the sages of Israel— ancient, medieval, and modern. For she will bring them forth to you now, whatever your religious heritage or present religious stance. This is Marcia Prager's gift to you, but even more precious is your own response; listen especially for that.

HOWARD LESNICK
Philadelphia, Pa.
November 1997

THE
PATH
OF
BLESSING

∞

You will seek Me
and you will find Me
when you search for Me
with all your heart.
And I will be found by you,
says יהוה.

—JEREMIAH 29:13–14

I was ready to be sought by those who did not ask for Me.
I was ready to be found by those who did not seek Me.
I said:"Here am I! Here am I!"

—ISAIAH 65:1

Introduction

❧

One summer evening after a Jewish women's retreat, I was invited to have dinner with one of the participants and her family. In our brief pre-dinner conversation her husband, Stan, spoke of his years of Buddhist practice—such a welcome refuge from the intrusively demanding yet vacant formulas of his Jewish upbringing. He had only recently begun to re-explore Jewish practice, he said, but it wasn't until dinner began that I learned why. We sat at the table and when the food was served, everybody looked at me: I was, after all, a rabbi, and, well, wasn't I supposed to say something?

Everyone waited. I looked around, absorbing the goodness of the people gathered at the table. With a deep breath I reached toward the basket of warm dinner rolls and lifted it up, closing my eyes to be alone with the sensations. Steamy-hot, just-baked bread.

I inhaled its warm sweetness. For just a moment it seemed that I held the fertile earth sprouting ripening wheat and saw the dough rising in an extravagant explosion of yeast. My fingertips touched the hot loaves. I sang: *"Barukh Ata Adonay, Eloheynu Melekh Ha'Olam, ha'motzi lechem min ha'aretz.* A Fountain of Blessings are You, Source of Life of all the Worlds, Source of the nourishment that is this bread, which You bring forth from the earth." We shared the bread around the table, and then Stan spoke.

"I grew up so angry!" he said. "All these blessings, these *brakhas* and prayers that I had to memorize. Always some rote formula to recite, another phrase to mumble. When I finally discovered Buddhism, it was such a relief. I embraced meditation and cultivated a practice of insight and mindfulness. It was only because of my deepening relationship with Judy that I began to be anywhere near practicing Jews again. But there was the same obsessive-compulsive stuff that I hated before. Every time they used something or saw something or ate something, there was another interruption and another mumble. It was so annoying. I was so grateful to be past that.

"One day, I don't remember what I was doing, it hit me! I was with someone and he stopped what he was doing to make a *brakha.* Like you just did. Suddenly I got it! All those years cultivating mindfulness and I didn't see. Making a *brakha,* the act of blessing, it IS a mindfulness practice. Mindfulness is what blessing IS."

We were quiet. Then we all grinned. I began to speak about exploring the Jewish spiritual practice of blessing ... and why I wanted to write this book.

--⦿--

A simple Hebrew blessing is a powerful thing—a one-minute, deeply meditative exercise exploring the nature of the Creative Force we call God and the dynamic relationship between God, human consciousness, and the unfolding universe. Far from a mindless mumble, each word of a Hebrew blessing is crafted to touch deep centers of awareness and receptivity within us. Each word is a stepping-stone inviting us to explore a rich treasury of images and associations.

Blessing offers us a personal consciousness-raising practice, a spiritual adventure bringing sensitivity and gratitude into the foreground of our lives. While we all have moments when a blessing rises spontaneously to our lips, the path of blessing can become a way of life.

Through the practice of blessing we develop an ever-deepening receptivity to the abundant love and joy flowing through Creation. We learn to accept that love, absorb it into our souls, and offer it back to the source with joy. In this way we come to feel the Presence of God move within us and through us. The result is bliss.

Blessing is not a recently invented practice. From biblical times to the present day, Jews have used blessings to consecrate the moments of our lives. We bless our students, our teachers, our children; we praise God with blessings for our bodies and our souls, for waking up, for walking upright, for our freedom, for our food from earth and tree, for our clothing and our livelihood, for breath, for vision, for guidance, for strength, for the wonders of nature, for the privilege of learning Torah and of serving God through sacred action. And the list doesn't end there.

In the texts of the Bible we find the earliest blessings of our fathers and mothers, passed from generation to generation. With the destruction of the Temple in Jerusalem in the 70th year of the Common Era, the system of sacrifices and offerings performed by the Temple priests (the *Kohanim*) came to an end. Surviving rabbis and scholars began a comprehensive reconstruction of all aspects of Jewish life. To the traumatized and despairing populace, the rabbis taught a revolutionary message: Prayer would now be offered in the temple of the heart. Together the rabbis labored to formulate the wording and order of daily prayer.

Over the course of many generations, blessings were given formal shape in language reflecting the emerging rabbinic attitude that prayer and learning could replace the Temple service as our people's living link to God. Between the first and sixth centuries of the Common Era, the vast record of Jewish law and lore we call the Talmud was compiled. Here we find detailed accounts of the discussions and debates between early teachers and their students about the content, structure, and meaning of blessing, and the patterns of prayer. For a thousand years and more, our prayers and blessings have traveled with us through all the continents of our dispersion, ancient words sung with the melodies and inflections of different lands.

Now we live in the midst of a new revolution. We have, as a people, passed through another time of destruction and emerged alive in a world offering different challenges and possibilities. Though still reeling from the grief and anguish of the destruction,

we turn to face a future holding the promise of miraculous trans-
formations. It is a critical time. A time in which our actions have
far-reaching consequences for life on our planet. We live in a world
that, as Rabbi Arthur Waskow has written, "is shaking underfoot:
where women and men are equal, the ghetto walls are gone, and even
great national boundaries are porous to poisonous air and water."
As we reject life-threatening ideologies of privilege and power, we
are called to envision and manifest new patterns of relationship
with one another and the earth.

For many of us, hierarchical structures of authority, including
many entrenched rabbinic patterns, no longer serve. Old forms
shatter and new forms arise to guide our steps. As women's voices
join equally with men's on the center stage of Jewish life, fresh rituals and blessings are being created to express women's experience
of the sacred. We bring new questions to our ancient stories, and
in the spiritual teachings of our ancestors discover rich and evoca-
tive landscapes of meaning.

Together we seek the courage and skill to heal the traumas of
the past and become healers in a re-imagined future to which we
offer Torah and our new-and-ancient blessings teaching life in harmony with the rhythms of a sacred world.

Each spiritual path has its own gifts. As a rabbi, teacher, and guide,
I have had the great joy of rooting myself in the ancient wisdom
of my people. In this book, when I refer to Jewish teaching as "our
people's teachings," my intention is not to exclude you if you are
not a Jew, but to speak to you from a Jewish context, which I am
inviting you to share. As a seeker, I have found soul-nourishing

insights enriching my journey on other paths. I am aware that Judaism has not always been well taught, with the result that both Jews and non-Jews have been deprived of access to it. Thus in this book I am speaking to anyone who wishes to cultivate the practice of blessing.

Because we want to enter as fully as possible into the spiritual wisdom embedded in the Hebrew, I use the original Hebrew vocabulary. Hebrew words and the teachings they offer are often vastly dissimilar from their common English translations. As we uncover deeper layers of meaning, new worlds of insight will open before us.

The Hebrew *Aleph-Beyt*

ALEPH	BEYT/ VEYT	GIMMEL	DALET	HEY	WAW	ZAYIN	CHET	TET
א	ב	ג	ד	ה	ו	ז	ח	ט
silent letter	Has sound of B or V	Has sound of G	Has sound of D	Has sound of H	Has sound of W (V in modern Hebrew)	Has sound of Z	Has sound of gutteral CH	Has sound of T
1	2	3	4	5	6	7	8	9
YOD	KAF/ KHAF	LAMED	MEM	NUN	SAMEKH	AYIN	PEY/ FEY	TZADI
י	כ	ל	מ	נ	ס	ע	פ	צ
Has sound of Y	Has sound of K or guttural KH	Has sound of L	Has sound of M	Has sound of N	Has sound of S	silent letter	Has sound of P or F	Has sound of TZ
10	20	30	40	50	60	70	80	90
KOF	REYSH	SIN/ SHIN	TAV	FINAL KHAF	FINAL MEM	FINAL NUN	FINAL FAY	FINAL TZADI
ק	ר	ש	ת	ך	ם	ן	ף	ץ
Has sound of K	Has sound of R	Has sound of S or SH	Has sound of T	Has sound of KH at the end of a word	Has sound of M at the end of a word	Has sound of N at the end of a word	Has sound of F at the end of a word	Has sound of TZ at the end of a word
100	200	300	400					

This alphabet chart is a guide to the Hebrew words and letters
you will encounter throughout this book.

When you feel a lack of understanding,
And your creativity declines
Run to the hidden spring!

The higher waters will refresh you,
And you will blossom.
God's blessing will return to you.
You will become like a gushing spring,
Like a river that does not cease.

—RAV ABRAHAM ISAAC KOOK

Live and take delight in all that is good,
Ascend,
Rise higher and higher!

—RAV ABRAHAM ISAAC KOOK

The Spiritual Practice
of *Brakhot*

❦

The tradition of blessing is woven into a larger matrix of Jewish spiritual practice informing the whole of life. It is also set in the larger context of *kedusha,* sacredness or holiness. Twice in Torah our people hear the command: "Be *kadosh*": "Be holy!" "Be sacred beings!" Our people's entire spiritual endeavor—all of Torah, all the law, all the praise, all the songs, all the prayers, blessings, and sacrifices—can be seen as a response to that call: "Be sacred beings, be *kadosh.*"

Our quest is to discern what that call means. How can one be *kadosh?* We hear in Proverbs the words of King Solomon: *"B'khol d'rakhekha daeyhu."* "In each of your ways, know God." We wonder how we can accomplish this. Our ways are those of human beings living in the world. We wake up; we go to sleep; we drink; we wash; we work; we buy and sell; we play; we pray; we have relationships;

we do laundry, take care of our children and our parents. . . . Know the source of holiness in ALL our ways? Bring *kedusha*, the sacred, into EVERY aspect of our lives? Is this not an impossible challenge?

If every aspect of our existence is an opportunity to experience God, how shall we live when we discover that God permeates all, from the galactic to the microscopic? How shall we respond—personally, as a society, as a species—when we begin to understand not only our lives but all existence as a sacred gift?

At times such *kedusha*, such a sense of the sacred, actually seems within our reach. We all have moments in which we are jolted out of our habitual anxiety, when we surrender control and let go of self-conscious judgments. In those moments we can just "be." We can feel refreshingly open, clear, and complete. Our mental clutter and confusions fall away, and we remember with great joy our oneness with all that is. At such moments the whole universe dances inside us!

In Hebrew this gentle attunement is called *mochin d'gadlut*—literally, "big mind," expanded consciousness—moments in which our hearts open to awe, wonder, and infinite possibility. In *mochin d'gadlut*, we are filled with God and every moment is a miracle unfolding.

We strive to hold on to this expansiveness of spirit. But it is difficult, and all too easily we slide back into the more limited spiritual condition of *mochin d'katnut*, "little mind," constricted consciousness. Accustomed to layers of distress, disappointments, and boredom, we "get by." We discover that we can avoid being hurt by diminishing our capacity to feel.

As we gradually become numb to both joy and pain, our lives appear manageable. This is the condition described as *galut*, alienation and exile from God. When we look at small children, we see their sense of wonder, their openness to the miraculous. But we notice, as we grow habituated to the world and its daily pressures, that our own moments of ecstatic delight diminish. When we allow all the daily miracles to be passed by, our openness to the abundance of divine blessing withers. We realize we have traded away our own aliveness and we long to find our way back. How strongly we need to counteract those dulling life pressures.

And still more! In order to nourish *kedusha,* any spiritual endeavor not only must act as an antidote to the dulling circumstances of life and keep alive our three-year-old's sense of wonder, it must also actively develop our awareness and sensitivity and nurture a maturation of consciousness.

This is the path of blessing.

The Hebrew word for blessing is ברכה *brakha* (plural ברכות *brakhot,* or sometimes, more colloquially, *brakhas*). The Jewish practice of blessing derives from our tradition's desire to promote joy and appreciation, wonder and thankfulness, amazement and praise. A *brakha* is, we might say, a kind of "gratitude yoga" we can employ not only day to day but moment to moment. It is in itself not at all strenuous. It doesn't require a *minyan,* the quorum of ten worshippers; it doesn't require travel; it doesn't require that we have any accoutrements or a special mantra or that we become a yogi, an adept, a *tzaddik,* or a buddha. It merely asks us to engage in a moment of delayed gratification, using the respite as an opportunity for something else to occur.

Just as every seventh day we separate out Shabbos, a sabbath, in order to remove ourselves from the physical work of the world, dedicating time to the work of the soul, so in making a *brakha* we separate out time before we consume, use, or enjoy something of the world in order to create a space where something other than thoughtless appropriation can unfold. As we grow in the path of blessing, we open to a more expansive way of being. Through blessing, we uncover the infinitely abundant Presence of God in even the smallest action.

Jewish tradition teaches that the simple action of a *brakha* has a cosmic effect, for a *brakha* causes *shefa*, the "abundant flow" of God's love and goodness, to pour into the world. Like a hand on the faucet, each *brakha* turns on the tap.

How delicious it is to live in God's goodness. Too often we walk uncaring and unconscious through our jobs and lives, oblivious to the love that surrounds us and is us. When, however, we live in the abundant flow, we know ourselves to be loved and supported unconditionally. Only then do we become free both to receive and to give fully.

Each acknowledgment of divine abundance cycles more blessing into the world. Thus all of life is enriched. Jewish consciousness carries a deep awareness that in order for the cycles to continue—whether those of an individual human life, community life, the seasons, or the universe—they need to be nourished. When we fail to cultivate a practice of appreciation as potent as our capacity to appropriate, we become despoilers, destroying both ourselves and the whole. When we use the world as if it belongs to us, we use it as we would a possession. The practice of blessing

helps us see that consuming without returning the gift of our conscious awareness makes us in a way like thieves.

In the first book of the Talmud, *Brakhot,* a detailed record of
early rabbinic teachings on blessing and prayer, one teacher
unabashedly exclaims, "Anyone who derives pleasure from this
world without a *brakha* is stealing from God!"

Another rabbi goes even further. "Each of us," he says, "will
be called to give account for the innocent delights of the world
which our eyes saw, but which we didn't let our mouths taste.
However, one who delights in this world without a *brakha* is like a
robber, because the *brakha* is what causes the continuation of the
divine flow of *shefa* into the world. [All of creation is fashioned of
sparks of divinity, and so] when the *brakha* is offered with directed
awareness and purposeful intention, we avoid becoming destructive
agents who selfishly hoard the sparks of divine energy in the food.
By blessing the Source of the fruit/food . . . we purify and release
the sparks back into the life-sustaining flow of holiness."

A *brakha* completes our energy-exchange with God. We are partners in a sacred cycle of giving and receiving in which we are not
only "on the take." When we offer our blessings, we raise up sparks
of holiness, releasing the God-light housed in our world back to its
Source. We receivers become givers, and the nurturing flow is sustained. When, on the other hand, we receive but fail to give, we
become clogged, sick, and destructive. When we fail to praise, it is
we who suffer. Without gratitude we become bored and depressed.
This teaching, so fundamental to the Jewish practice of blessing, is
movingly reflected as well in the poetry of Rumi, the Sufi poet:
"Your depression is connected to your insolence and refusal to

praise! Whoever feels himself walking on the path and refuses to praise—that man or woman steals from others every day—is a shoplifter!"

Imagine if at every moment we each embraced the world as the gift it is: An apple is a gift; the color pink is a gift; the blue sky is a gift; the scent of honeysuckle is a gift. Hidden in every experience is a gift, obligating us to heart-filled appreciation, to songs of gratitude. We are called not merely to notice casually now and then that something is special and nice but to sustain and deepen a profound and sustained gratitude. Indeed, the more we acknowledge our gratefulness, the more we temper our tendency to be users, despoilers, arrogant occupiers.

We are on our way to *kedusha*.

Blessing God

Because the word *brakha* is usually translated "blessing," it can be valuable to begin our journey by investigating some of the questions this translation raises.

What does it mean to "bless"?

In common folk practice, when someone sneezes, we may say "Bless you." The expression has its roots in the hope that the words will ward off evil. To bless someone is to wish the person good fortune or to pray that Divine Providence will be favorable. But why, then, would someone offer a blessing to God? The notion seems absurd; God doesn't need blessing and anyway, how could a human being bring God good fortune?

Blessing implies a transfer of intention, hopefulness, or awareness from a source to a recipient. If I bless you, I seek to move something of myself toward you. I want you to feel more confidence, more hopefulness, to become richer in some way. I am offering you something by blessing you. When we experience God as a Source of blessing, a Source of hope, confidence, and empowerment, we feel ourselves enriched. But the questions remain: Should we have to give hope and confidence to God? If not, what is it that I am moving toward God?

When we offer "blessing" to the Source of Blessing, we offer our gratitude not only for a particular gift but for the opportunity to experience our connection with the whole of life. Our *brakha* opens us to the *shefa* of divine goodness moving through us, filling us and flowing back to God. We partake of the world and are invited to experience God within everything.

This practice conveys a radical teaching: Neither the food we eat nor anything we find in the world is as inert as it may seem! Becoming aware of this takes us almost by surprise, yet at the same time seems more like a recollection of something we have always known. Discovering God's aliveness in our world can feel as if a veil has been lifted and a joyous clarity returned. Ironically, our minds usually conceal this perception. We create mental constructs objectifying the world and obscuring its Godliness. On the path of blessing, we are reminded that the whole world is an expression of divine energy.

The sixteenth-century Kabbalist Rabbi Moshe Cordovero said, "The essence of divinity is found in every single thing—nothing but It exists. Since It causes every thing to be, no thing can live by anything else.... Do not say, 'This is a stone and not God.' God forbid! Rather, all existence is God and the stone is a thing pervaded by divinity."

Rabbi Menachem Nachum of Chernobyl, gifted disciple of the Baal Shem Tov (the eighteenth-century mystical master who inspired the Eastern European Jewish spiritual revival known as Hasidism) proclaimed: "God is garbed in everything! No place is empty of God!" Regarding the verse from Isaiah, "All the earth is filled with God's Glorious-Presence," he taught, "Glorious-Presence, that means garments." That is, the whole earth is filled with God's garments! All physicality is an enrobing of Divinity, each subatomic particle of Creation housing a spark of God.

The flow of divine energy into the world is sometimes compared to the flow of sap in a tree. The limbs of the tree are the pathways through which the life-giving God-energy courses. One word for "sap" in Hebrew, *s'raf*, literally means "burning energy" or "fire," alluding to the sparks of sacred fire within everything.

Rabbi Isaac Luria, the great sixteenth-century master of Kabbalah—Jewish mystical teaching—urged us to see every physical object or being as sustained by the spark of holiness within it. When we eat, our bodies extract vitamins and minerals, but, he reminded us, it is not these that keep our souls alive! The human soul, he taught, recognizes and extracts the holy spark and from the spark is truly nourished.

When we walk the path of blessing, we begin to recognize the presence of these holy sparks in everything and everyone around us. Day by day the world becomes more alive, more magical, more miraculous! We partake of its gifts and with joy we lift up the holy sparks to fly freely back to God. With each *brakha* we also grow in awareness of our own miraculous soul-spark: God garbed in the essence of our own being.

The kabbalistic work *Pri Etz Hadar, Fruit of the Goodly Tree*, teaches us in these beautiful words how to focus our intention as we prepare to offer a *brakha:*

> Holy One of Blessing
> may it come to pass
> that through the sacred power
> of the fruit we are now eating and blessing,
> (while we meditate on the secret of the flow of
> Divine Energy upon which they depend),
> that the Divine Flow of Blessing abundantly fill them.
> May the flow never cease,
> so that all will grow
> from the beginning of the year until its end,
> for abundance and blessing, for good life,
> for fulfillment and peace.

Sending blessing back to the Source of Blessing is far more than just a "thank you card" of gratitude or praise. With our *brakha* we participate in the flow of divinity through the world. Now let us see precisely how the words of a Hebrew *brakha* assist us in cultivating those qualities of the soul that are requisite for this work.

∞

Apprehend God in all things,
for God is in all things.
Every creature is a word of God.

—MEISTER ECKHART

Language and God

❦

Hebrew as a Language of Creation

The individual words of a *brakha* are designed to activate centers of awareness deep in the psyche. They are not a "Rub-a-dub-dub, thanks for the grub, yeah, God" (although even this may be better than nothing). To fully comprehend a *brakha*, we must first understand Jewish teachings about language, because the meaning of Hebrew words is informed by the unique role that language plays in the process of creation.

Jewish tradition invites us to approach the Hebrew language in a way unfamiliar to most speakers of Western languages. Just as the Infinite Light of God can be found radiating from within nature and all living things, so too we can find that light within the Hebrew letters. Each letter is also a "garment." Hebrew letters are like atoms of creation energy, Hebrew words like molecules. Each letter contains a unique energy signature drawn from the first primordial light, a resonance of God's original act of creating. Each letter comes from God and guides us back toward God. Each holds a ray of the brilliance of creation, a vibration of the primal sound spoken into being by God "in the beginning." So it is here at the beginning that we embark on our journey into sacred speech.

Many Jewish mystical teachings about language are embedded in the story of the beginning. In the beginning God . . . "says": יהי "Yehi!" "Let there be!," or perhaps better, "Exist! . . ." and whoosh, Creation manifests! The action is dramatic, but it is easy to overlook the more subtle implications of this simple sentence. Once we pause here, we see something intriguing. Creation is correlated with speaking! How should we understand this? Is there a giant Superbeing literally speaking? Or is Torah pointing us toward something deeper?

To create *midrash* is to dive into the stories of Torah and bring hidden meanings to the surface. For centuries Jewish mystics and kabbalists have explored the earliest stories of Torah for clues about the origin of the universe and the mystery we call Creation. From their teachings we discern that God's speaking Creation into existence must be understood as a metaphor for a vastly larger creative process. Suffused with desire to pour love and goodness into a responsive universe, God "speaks" Creation into existence by emanating surges of divine energy from within God's innermost Being. One could perhaps say that God "ex-presses" Creation.

Consider the process of speech in your own body. You want to say something, to offer your feelings or ideas. The wanting causes an energy to rise up within you. Your diaphragm rises, your stomach muscles tighten, and your breath waits in expectancy. Your body tenses lightly as it prepares to ex-press. Express what? Your SELF. To speak is to ex-press yourself. God "speaks" and "ex-presses" or "presses out" God's SELF. From deep within the Infinite-Core-of-Being, wave after wave of energy pours forth. God, the conscious source, "speaks" creation into existence by expressing God's Self, and from deep within God all the letter energies of creation flow into the world.

Material existence is born and evolves, drawn toward an exceptional possibility: that Creation, emanating from the One Conscious Light, may itself achieve consciousness.

Then God formed the human from the dusty earth
and breathed into it "Living Soul/Breath," and it became
a conscious life.

—Genesis 2:7

Human consciousness awakens and turns to face God, awakens and links with God through language.

The mythic story of the first conscious being, the androgynous human in the Garden of Eden, offers us a glimpse into that once-and-future time when a creature in the material world lived utterly present to the flow of God's creative energies as they became clothed, first in letters and then in physical forms. This mystical tale of Eden invites us to imagine a time when humans were so new, so unarmored, so open to the energies of Creation, that we could "hear" divine "speech," the Creation-vibrations in all things, and articulate those vibrations as sound. The miracle is that the newly created earthling has both the mind and the vocal cords to express Creation-awareness as words with meaning!

Perhaps you recall that the first task given the *Adam* (the Hebrew for "earthling") in the Garden was to name all other creatures. In a popular trivialization of that story, we might imagine an earthling standing in the Garden as the animals pass in procession before him, and assigning them names the way one might name a pet. But the *Adam* is actually engaged in a far more momentous undertaking. By naming, the *Adam* participates actively in the project of Creation, articulating with human syllables the constituent God-energies calling those creatures into being and formulating their uniqueness. Each creature's "name" is its essence, its combination of letters spoken into being by God. In order to give voice to their names, the earthling must be completely permeable to each creature's essence. Only then can that creature offer the *Adam* its energies to be articulated in human syllables as its name.

As creatures whose consciousness is multilayered, who are "aware that we are aware" and can articulate at least some of that awareness, we are able to give voice to the energies of Creation. We are physical beings, yet we can sense the spiritual and physical energies within all things. As we learn to resonate with those energies, we become like tuning forks, imprinting God's creative energy on our awareness and expressing it in our lives.

When Genesis says, "whatever the *Adam* called every living creature, that was its name," it is describing not the imposition of a human label, but an act of discernment, a recognition of something essential about each creature. Part of our purpose as human beings is to apprehend the spiritual nature of each aspect of

Creation. In this way we link ourselves to the original *Adam*. The Torah story teaches us that we can discern the presence of God in every thing and every creature of our world and express that awareness as language!

You may want to pause here, and perhaps take a deep breath. This is heady stuff. We are being asked to understand language itself in an entirely new way. If you have imagined that speech could be casual and inconsequential, think again! Language can connect us to the moment-by-moment process through which God creates all that exists. We can use our power of speaking in a revolutionary way—to speak ourselves and the world toward holiness.

Once we begin to understand the power of language, we can grasp the traditional Jewish idea that by giving voice to our thoughts we participate with God in Creation. Language is an outpouring of intention and the desire to create. Therefore, while a *brakha* can be thought silently, the tradition asks us to articulate our blessings aloud. When our mouths speak our thoughts and when our ears hear what our mouths have said, more senses are involved. The entire person is engaged. One might say that in each expression of energy, a new reality has been created.

Jewish tradition asks us to understand the Hebrew language as a particularly potent link to the flow of God into Creation. Creation is happening every moment. Each Hebrew word is a "name," called again and again by God, and as we speak, also by us. Through the words and the letters we utter, we join in the process of Creation. We therefore craft our blessings so that each word and syllable resonate with the fullness of God's Presence.

Through our blessings we become ever more conscious beings whose lives dance with holy sparks.

Sacred Language and the Dilemma of Translation

The twentieth-century movement to revitalize Hebrew envisioned a Jewish spiritual renaissance in which the ancient tongue would again be the vehicle of our people's creative expression. Today Hebrew is once more a living language, carrying as part of its inheritance a wealth of religious vocabulary. Yet even for many fluent Israelis and certainly for most Americans, it remains a spiritually opaque language.

With the collapse of a fundamentally religious context for the totality of life (a legacy of modernity simultaneously sad and valuable) we have for the most part lost the view of language as a repository of profound teaching about the nature of the sacred. In the West, language functions predominantly as a utilitarian vehicle, each word conveying a discrete and limited "byte" of information. The lexicon is huge and communication is rapid.

But Hebrew is a *lashon kadosh,* a sacred language. The Holy One "speaks" Creation into existence, so that each letter and word is resonant with divinity. How little of this sensibility is carried into English!

In English, the ten words that open a Hebrew *brakha*—"*Barukh Ata Adonay, Eloheynu Melekh Ha'Olam, asher kid'shanu b'mitzvotav v'tzivanu*"—are most often translated: "Blessed art Thou, O Lord our God, King of the Universe, who has sanctified us by Thy commandments and commanded us to..." Happily the Hebrew expresses something far deeper than this translation would suggest. As we shall see, there are few English words that fully convey what the Hebrew expresses. It is not simply that there is a better translation, although there is. It is that the very idea of "translation" as usually understood is inadequate.

This is true because Hebrew is a very different kind of language from English. It has simultaneously different structure, nature, and purpose. One way I describe the differences is to say that Hebrew is a "depth" language; it uses fewer words than English and requires each word to carry more information and thus greater depth of meaning.

Like leaves and branches growing from a tree trunk, most Hebrew words derive from what is called a root. Just as each leaf must be understood as a part, fed by the roots of the whole tree, individual Hebrew words cannot be fully understood without reference to their whole tree. The root stores all the meanings flowing into each one of the leaves. There are even implications in Hebrew words that do not necessarily operate at a conscious level.

All this complexity is very difficult to capture in English, and so the translation of sacred Hebrew is often a frustrating enterprise. Sometimes whole paragraphs of English can be insufficient to convey the meaning of a single Hebrew word. The lone word chosen generally conveys a sadly atrophied sense of the Hebrew. A century of stiff "hymnal" translation has further compounded the difficulty, leaving a legacy of theological distress for many of us. There are Hebrew words we know only in the context of traditional translations and the general Western worldview underlying them. The good news is that we can do much better!

As we engage each of the Hebrew words of blessing, we will also look at the individual letters, because each letter of the Hebrew *aleph-beyt* transmits divine energy into Creation. As we have said, words are the complex molecules, and letters the atomic "building blocks." Together the letters of the *aleph-beyt* are like a periodic chart of the "spiritual elements." Even their placement within that chart is revealing.

Furthermore, the letters are interactive. When they come together to form words, letters interact like elements in a chemical bond or like a sequence of genes in a DNA strand. The combination of letters forms the spiritual structure of the thing named.

That Hebrew letters have distinct spiritual meanings may seem startling, because there is no parallel in English. English letters are sound-symbols only: *A* and *B* do not intrinsically mean anything. Even if one could write out the sound of a letter phonetically, as if it were a word, an English letter is not a word. But Hebrew letters, just like hydrogen or helium in the periodic table of elements, have names that are words with meanings.

In addition, it is important to be aware that each Hebrew letter is also a number. Traditional Hebrew does not use Western (Arabic) numerals. Counting is done with letters. In fact, the Hebrew word for "telling," *sipur,* is also the word for "counting." Because letters have mathematical value, when one is spelling, one is also placing numbers in sequence. Thus there often are additional layers of meaning available when we pay attention to the numerical value of letters as we read. In a way, then, we don't "read" sacred Hebrew at all, we "decipher" it.

—◦◦◦◦—

Many Jews have learned to rattle off the opening words of a *brakha* as a perfunctory formula: *Barukh-Ata-Adonay-Eloheynu-Melekh-Ha'Olam-asher-kid'shanu-b'mitzvotav-v'tzivanu.* This often comes across like gobbledygook, reminiscent of "Ipledgeallegiancetotheflag," a phrase that has left millions of schoolchildren wondering what "dgeallegiance" is. Similarly, when learning the Hebrew formula, students are seldom taught the true inner meaning of the words.

The vocabulary of the standard English translation not only fails to speak to the fullness of the Hebrew but often evokes negative stereotypes, reminding us of royal despotism and conjuring up God as a distant sovereign issuing fearful "commandments." The translations are weighted toward imagery of oppression rather than of liberation, and have the ring of nineteenth-century prose that is no longer alive for us.

This simplistic approach to translation is all too often used in teaching religion to children. It is a common view that religious instruction is for children, and religious schools rarely progress in their theology beyond the pitch made to the youngest. Of course, even if we are taught by the most skilled and enlightened teachers, if our theological development ends at an early age we will be left with a spiritual vocabulary ill-equipped to meet complex adult demands. Theological skills and vocabulary should grow as we do. Poor teaching in childhood not only robs us of the desire to explore further, but can leave us unaware that there is a "further" to explore.

Most American Jews lack an ongoing, evolving engagement with mature, enlightened Jewish practice, or even any awareness that such a thing exists. For too many of us, all we have retained from Judaism, when we do need spiritual sustenance, are frozen, limited (or worse, harmful) images. We think this is all Judaism offers and we are angry. Our thirsty souls turn away, often to other traditions whose wisdom is more accessible. Sometimes those paths do offer the nourishment we need to stay alive and grow. And for some of us, paradoxically, that nourishment fuels our journey home.

We need an entirely new consciousness for teaching Jewish spiritual practice. When I work with adults tentatively re-exploring the Jewish path, and we begin to unfold the depth of imagery and teaching available, I am often aghast at how these adults have been cheated. But they need more than just another translation. We must paint anew the whole landscape arising from the ancient words as we add the colors of our new visions. As the great contemporary kabbalist Rav Abraham Isaac Kook proclaimed: "The old shall be made new and the new shall be made holy."

In this guidebook we will travel through each of the opening words of a *brakha*. We will examine the root of each word, the meanings conveyed by the individual letters, and even the significance of other words deriving from the letters, because this is all part of the constellation of meaning informing a blessing. We will treat each word as an activator of a center of God-awareness within the soul, so that as the word is articulated, it opens a new window of experience. As we will see, Hebrew is a rich symbolic language. When we travel into it as a sacred language, we embark on a kaleidoscopic journey into our people's quest to know God. On that journey we meet God moving toward us.

ברוך

One glorious chain of love,
of giving and receiving,
unites all things.
All things exist in continuous
reciprocal activity—
one for All, All for one.
None has power, or means, for itself;
Each receives only to give,
and gives only to receive, and finds therein
the fulfillment of the purpose of existence.

—RABBI SAMSON RAPHAEL HIRSCH

ברוך אתה יהוה אלהנו מלך העולם

A Fountain of Blessings

Barukh

ဗာ

The sequence of words in a Hebrew blessing is like a path of stepping-stones. Each word is a spiritual exercise. Taken together, the opening six words common to all *brakhot* are an invocation or an overture, announcing our intention to channel blessing and raise up sparks of holiness. The words prepare the path for our offering as a theater stage anticipates and makes space for a play. As we engage each of these words, we set the stage, raise the curtain, and bring up the spotlights.

We begin in the silence that precedes any sound or movement. Jewish tradition asks that we not say a *brakha* until we have quieted the mind and focused our attention on the blessing's purpose. "One should not toss a *brakha* from one's mouth," instructs the Talmud. The eleventh-century commentator Rashi adds: "A *brakha* should be said slowly and deliberately. Don't rush through as if you

31

are carrying a heavy burden and cannot wait to be free of it!" In quiet attentiveness we focus attention and allow an opening for mindfulness.

The Hebrew word for focused intention is *kavvanah*. When we quiet the mind and prepare to offer our *brakha* with *kavvanah*, we experience an inner shift redirecting our soul toward God. We are able to gently release anxieties, feeling gratitude for the gift of this moment and the holy sparks it contains. We may wish to ask for an easing of all blemishes of ego restricting our awareness in order to deepen our praise and allow any lingering alienation and separateness to disappear.

Begin the words of your *brakha* only when you feel ready, holding in your heart the desire that your *brakha* be for the sake of *kedusha*, the holiness of the world.

—◦◉◦—

The first word of a *brakha*, ברוך, pronounced *barukh*, is commonly translated "blessed." As we have seen, this translation can offer us a gateway to useful insight on the meaning of blessing. But let us look further. There is much more in the word *barukh*, encoded in the three consonants that form its root. Almost every Hebrew word is built on three core consonants called the root. Additional letters serve particular grammatical functions, or, as here, are simply vowel-holders like ו. In the word *barukh* the three root letters are: ברוך *BaRuKH*: ב *beyt*, ר *reysh*, and כ *khaf* (which is printed as ך when it appears at the end of a word). Each of these letters guides us toward a deeper understanding of the inner qualities cultivated by the practice of blessing as a way of life.

Each letter is unique but at the same time is part of a larger story. The position of each letter in the chart of the *aleph-beyt* is important, as well as its relationship with the letters appearing before and after it. We can treat the sequence of letters in the *aleph-beyt*, beginning with א *aleph* and ending with ת *tav*, as a Hebrew mythic tale in which each letter embodies a moment in the ongoing adventure of Creation. ב *Beyt*, the first letter of *barukh*, is the second letter of the *aleph-beyt*. We can glean the teachings offered by the letter *beyt* only after we have briefly visited its predecessor, *aleph*. (Later we will look at *aleph* more extensively for further teaching about the nature of the power we call God.)

The letter א *aleph* begins the narrative. Jewish mystical tradition teaches that Creation surfaced from deep within the Infinite Light of God. There in timeless unity, a primal impulse, a "desire to give," arose within the All. But the All was the One Pure God Light that is called *Ayn Sof,* "Without End." There was no space within "Without End" in which such giving could take place. There was only God. No time, no space. Yet the desire to give did not abate. It grew stronger and stronger. Then, with a surge of power and infinite longing, God contracted. God withdrew a point of God's pure essence, pulling back Self to create a space—an opening at first singular and dimensionless, then larger and yet larger—into which God might give, and within which a universe might be born.

For the infinite to generate the finite, the One must generate the possibility of "other" from within itself. For "other" to exist, Oneness must self-limit. God must create boundaries out of God's own substance so that difference becomes possible.

The letters tell the story. א *Aleph* is the Infinite, the All. *Aleph* is the *"Aluph"*: the First Principle, the Primary Reality beyond knowing; in Rumi's words, it is "the ocean at whose edge all footsteps disappear." It is from this infinite *aleph* unity—beyond human comprehension, the source of all existence—that all Creation begins its journey. Deep within the heart of the One, a movement, an urge, a desire grows, from which our spatial, temporal, and material universe swells.

Into an expanding cosmos God-light flares forth in a never-ceasing spiral of emanations birthing time and space, a universe of galaxies, stars, and planets, and our own earth—teeming with life. Out of the primal *aleph* unity emerges *olam ha'pirud*, the "World of Distinctions" or "World of Separations." This is the sphere of dimensionality and physicality in which we live.

ב Deep within the one infinite *aleph* light an urge for "other" emerges, a coalescing, containing energy expressed as the letter ב *beyt*, which means "house." God-energy flows into the unfolding universe and cools, condensing as garments or "housings" of matter and energy. The letter ב *beyt* offers us the opportunity to experience all of Creation—from the cosmic to the subatomic—as a house of God, a dwelling place of divinity.

The letter ב *beyt* teaches that the first act of Creation is the coming-into-existence of "dwelling within." In Genesis we read that the first creative expression of God is *"Yehi Or! Let there be light!"* Although the surface reading suggests that light was the first product of Creation, Jewish mystical tradition understands this light as an already cooled energy, already diminished from the One Infinite Light, already contained.

Within *beyt*, the endless light is progressively condensed and therefore also gradually concealed. What a paradox it is, that the full intensity of God's Light is concealed precisely so that beneficial light can be revealed! Without "housing," the infinite energy of Creation cannot manifest itself even as light, much less as life. The divine energy must dwell within in order for its creative potential to unfold.

It is in this context, teaches the Koznitzer Maggid, that our sages call God "The Holy One." In Hebrew, the word "holy," *kadosh*, also carries the meaning of "separate" or "distinct." The name "Holy One" can therefore suggest that "God separated from God's own Infinity in order to . . . dwell within finite physicality."

Creation embodies and radiates the Living Presence of God. A radical assertion! All physicality houses God! All reality, microscopic and galactic, is an in-dwelling, an in-being, an incarnation. All existence is a *beyt* of God. *Aleph* becomes *beyt*. God becomes world!

There is a special way Torah's use of the letter *beyt* invites us to explore one step further. In English the opening sentence of the Bible most commonly reads, "In the beginning . . ." We read this and discern that we are about to be told a story of the beginning of Creation, but we often move quickly past these words, treating them merely as a "once-upon-a-time." When we do this, we miss the story concealed in the Hebrew words.

The first word in Torah is בְּרֵאשִׁית *B'reishit*, "In the beginning." Thus בּ *beyt*, the *aleph-beyt*'s second letter, which we know means "house," or "dwelling," is the first letter of the Torah story of Creation. Jewish tradition teaches that no word or letter of Torah is ever to be passed over as random or circumstantial. The position and order of every word and letter are intentional. But if the letter-story of the unfolding of God's Oneness into the world begins with *aleph*, shouldn't we expect the story of Creation to begin with *aleph* as well?

We can understand the placement of ב *beyt* as truly purposeful and neither illogical nor accidental, if we consider its placement as the first letter of Torah to be an encoding of the unique perspective on Creation we have just described. Without ב *beyt*, without the housing-of-God in-the-world, there would be no world, no inquiry, and no storytellers, no "we" to speculate on the mythic drama of an *aleph*. The absolute infinite *aleph* oneness is the source of Creation and defies knowing. For created beings, Genesis begins only at the moment when Infinity creates Other. From the infinite א *aleph*-oneness, the Wholly One becomes the Holy One, creating "two-ness," other-ness: multiplicity and diversity. This is for us the true beginning. The letter whose numerical value is two seems to say, "From the One comes two. From two come the many. The story of abundance begins with ב *beyt!*"

For creation to occur, God's Oneness requires a house. א *Aleph* requires ב *beyt*. God requires a home, a vessel. You are one of those vessels. For every atom, every cell, of us is such a house, a dwelling-place of God. As we grow in this awareness of God dwelling within us, we can comprehend more deeply the holiness resident in all Creation. In every moment God fashions the world out of God's own Self. With *ahavah* and *ratzon*, love and desire, God condenses God's own light into everything-that-is in order to dwell within us.

We are invited to reflect upon all this when we pronounce the sound of the letter ב *beyt.*

ר *Reysh*, the next letter of *barukh*, means "head"; perhaps for our purposes we could even say "cranium." Its curve is the curve of the skull, the brain's container, for ר *reysh* holds the mind's store of wisdom and understanding. Recall the analogy of the Hebrew letters to the periodic table of the elements. In the periodic chart of the letters, ב *beyt* is two and ר *reysh* is two hundred. Their position on the same column of the chart aligns them in a family of letters conveying the meaning of "house" or "vessel." If two means "house," "dwelling," or "container," two hundred is two-ness or "container-ness" magnified, *beyt* energy brought to an even greater realization. Some call *reysh* the "cosmic container" because it is the fullest expression of two-ness in the *aleph-beyt*. It is spoken of as an exalted *beyt*, so that when we pronounce its sound we stretch even further our sense of God housed in the world.

כ/ך *Khaf*, meaning "cupped palms" open to receive, also suggests containment. (Because in Hebrew *f* and *p* are the same letter, it is interesting to speculate about the relationship between the English "cup" and the Hebrew *khaf*.) Cupped hands very naturally convey the symbolic meaning of holding, containing, and sheltering, so it may come as no surprise that the numerical value of the letter כ *khaf* is twenty. In the chart of letters it is placed right between ב *beyt* and ר *reysh*. Thus in the word ברוך *BaRuKH*, we find only those root letters whose numerical values are 2, 200, and 20. It is rare and exciting for a word to be made up of three root letters all from the same column. 222! When I see this, I sense we are being offered a word whose letters are like a beacon.

ALEPH	BEYT/ VEYT	GIMMEL	DALET	HEY	WAW	ZAYIN	CHET	TET
א	ב	ג	ד	ה	ו	ז	ח	ט
silent letter	Has sound of B or V	Has sound of G	Has sound of D	Has sound of H	Has sound of W (V in modern Hebrew)	Has sound of Z	Has sound of gutteral CH	Has sound of T
1	2	3	4	5	6	7	8	9
YOD	KAF/ KHAF	LAMED	MEM	NUN	SAMEKH	AYIN	PEY/ FEY	TZADI
י	כ	ל	מ	נ	ס	ע	פ	צ
Has sound of Y	Has sound of K or guttural KH	Has sound of L	Has sound of M	Has sound of N	Has sound of S	silent letter	Has sound of P or F	Has sound of TZ
10	20	30	40	50	60	70	80	90
KOF	REYSH	SIN/ SHIN	TAV	FINAL KHAF	FINAL MEM	FINAL NUN	FINAL FAY	FINAL TZADI
ק	ר	ש	ת	ך	ם	ן	ף	ץ
Has sound of K	Has sound of R	Has sound of S or SH	Has sound of T	Has sound of KH at the end of a word	Has sound of M at the end of a word	Has sound of N at the end of a word	Has sound of F at the end of a word	Has sound of TZ at the end of a word
100	200	300	400					

The letters *beyt, reysh,* and *khaf* form a column equaling 222.

As I begin a *brakha* and slowly pronounce the word ברוך *barukh*, I feel each letter calling to me: "Clear out your mental clutter! Open up! Fill with so much light that you overflow! The letters בר ך *beyt reysh khaf* call me to join in a sacred stretch. I breathe deeply and find an inner space of sweet stillness. I empty myself out so that I can be fully present, fully available to receive the *shefa* of divine goodness.

Once at a restaurant I sat near a decorative copper fountain, in the form of a delicate tree with many leaves. Its water percolated from a thin pipe in the center and splashed out the top. Each leaf, like a cupped *khaf*, collected water and overflowed, spilling into the leaf below. The fountain tinkled as drops descended, splashing from leaf to leaf, from *khaf* to *khaf*. At the base, a well gathered the fallen drops into a pool, circulating them back to the top to begin their descent once more.

This little fountain was only restaurant decor, but it offered an "aha!" moment for me: an enactment of a fountain of blessing, each leaf a *beyt, reysh,* and *khaf*. I saw that we and God are such a fountain, the cupped hands of our souls like the upturned fountain leaves, filling with God and pouring out our songs of prayer and praise.

As I fill from the ever-flowing well, I too can give without lacking. The Holy One of Blessing is the fountain from which light and love pour, renewing Creation at every moment. In Hebrew prayer, God is praised every morning as the One who, with goodness, makes "the beginning" anew each moment. The fountain of divine goodness is pouring out into Creation at every moment! All we are asked to do is to be aware that we are leaves on the fountain, endlessly filling and pouring. Our melody is a song of astonishment and praise: *Kol ha'neshama t'hallel Yah!* sings the Psalmist. "Every soul-breath praises God!"

Our *brakhot,* our blessings, are like pumps circulating the water from the pool back up to the top where the *shefa,* the abundant flow of goodness, continues to pour down. In this way, we receivers also are givers. Each particle of creation is both a receptive vessel and an active channel. We humans are self-aware vessels who can know that our souls, like the leaves on the fountain, must be kept open if we are to continue to receive and pour out. We have the capacity to make a conscious choice to be vessels of blessing and keep the fountain flowing.

Jewish tradition teaches that the flow of *shefa* can become constricted by "kinks in the tubing" arising from destructive human action. From the Source, the desire is to flow without ceasing. But precisely because of the unfailing generosity of that *shefa,* we are in danger of taking its flow for granted or trying to keep it for ourselves, arrogantly imagining we have dominion over all things and are the source of our own sustenance.

By beginning with the word *barukh,* a *brakha* seeks to jolt us into awareness. Perhaps, by offering us the chain of letters which form 222, *barukh* is saying "keep it going!" so that the flow of divine goodness will not dissipate, but move consciously within us, so we become committed participants in that rhythmic flow.

It is therefore exquisite that the Hebrew word for "fountain" or "pool," *breikha,* derives from the same three letters as does *barukh.* Far from being simply a metaphor or a clever image, the notion of a fountain of blessings is present within the very root of the word *barukh!* For this reason I usually translate *barukh* as "a fountain of blessings" rather than "blessed," to acknowledge *barukh* in its fullest meaning: "You are the *Breikha*—Fountain, Source of all *brakhot*."

When I pronounce the sounds of the word *barukh*, I feel myself a leaf on that fountain, turning my receptive soul like cupped hands to face the Source of blessing and offering my fullness as a gift from the Source to the next soul. As we become practitioners of blessing, each word of our *brakha* begins to do its work in expanding our consciousness. We can allow the word *barukh* to gently stretch our tight soul musculature. The word *barukh* can "reelasticize" our souls so that we can accommodate the *shefa*, the flow of hope and love and goodness that is the Divine.

In the Jewish spiritual tradition we have many stories of the power of blessing. To be in the presence of a true master of this practice, a *baal brakhot*, is to experience the living power of the words and the holy sparks they raise up. Many tales are told of teachers whose blessings could transport them into the highest realms of consciousness.

The young Kabbalist Rabbi Avraham Ha'Malakh ("Avraham the Angel") was known as the holy master who could never finish a *brakha*. Seated at the table, surrounded by his students, he would raise a glass of wine and begin to sing, *"Barukh . . ."* His face would begin to glow as he would pass into other realms. His students might hear him murmur, "Ahhh, . . . *baruuuukh . . . ,*" and they would have to shake him to get him to come back to finish the blessing!

How powerful each of these words can be. Each word of a *brakha* can be said with such *kavvanah* that our whole way of being is transformed. Once we know its deep meaning, each word does its work to help the soul open.

Jewish tradition teaches that we should be able to say one hundred *brakhot* a day. Our lives should be so rich and varied, so filled with awareness, that our souls will want to stretch one hundred times a day! How many of us experience, in our daily lives, a hundred "wows"? What a treat it could be to feel so alive to the world that each taste, each scent, each glimpse of the world's beauty, would move us to exclaim at the miracle of it all. Imagine a day filled with a hundred wonders. Does this seem beyond reach? It needn't be. Each moment offers us more gifts than we imagine. We wake up and are alive; we have miraculous bodies; we are free; we have minds that learn and hearts that love. We can taste and feel. Our lives are a banquet of sensations. Take a moment and remember: the tang of tangerine, the sensuous sweetness of milk chocolate, spicy cinnamon tea, hearty whole-grain bread, biscuits dripping butter and honey, pasta with parmesan and garlic, cold watermelon on a hot summer day. We open our eyes and see astounding colors—the infinitely deep blue sky above us, and a rainbow palette of every bold and subtle hue around us. We see the first flowering trees of spring and dandelion weeds affirming life in the cracks of asphalt. Hidden wonders lie even in the most mundane tasks of our lives, from washing dishes in slithery suds to pink baby-bottoms at diaper-change time. When we want to acknowledge the miracle of these moments, to remember them, to log them, we can do this with a *brakha*.

Berekh/Knee and *Anavah*/Humility

There is yet another branch of the *beyt-reysh-khaf* tree we can visit. This new word helps us discern the underlying emotional requirement, perhaps one might say the "psychospiritual precondition," we must cultivate in order to be true vessels of blessing. It is not enough merely to know that the word *brakha* asks us to do a soul stretch and be a vessel. We cannot simply call to the soul and say, "OK, stretch now!" We must learn *how* to stretch. I ask myself how I can prepare for this stretch. What qualities can I cultivate to do it well? Is there a soul-exercise I could practice regularly? Can I make myself a supple enough vessel that when my soul hears the word *barukh,* it knows what to do?

Another *beyt-reysh-khaf* word offers us key insight into becoming vessels of blessing. That word is ברך *berekh,* which means "knee." Perhaps this seems incongruous? We have been speaking of blessings, abundant flow, and fountains. Why "knee"?

Allow yourself a few moments to think about this. You may make the connection yourself.

You might say, "The knee is a flexible joint and suggests the flexibility we need to allow blessing to move through us." True. But let's go further. There is one knee-flex particularly pertinent: we can kneel! *Berekh* brings kneeling into our discussion. What does it mean to kneel, and what does kneeling have to do with blessing?

We must acknowledge that there is a shadow side to some words. Kneeling has been used throughout history as a sign of subjugation and degradation. I remember from *The King and I,* a favorite Broadway musical of my childhood, the English governess Anna chastising the autocratic king of Siam: "Toads, toads!" she rails at him, "All of your people are toads!"

> Crawling around on your elbows and knees,
> Eating the dust of the road! . . .

Yes, Your Majesty; No, Your Majesty . . .
Give us a kick, if you please, Your Majesty.
Give us a kick, if you would, Your Majesty.
Oh! That was good, Your Majesty!

I recall, even as a child, feeling so grateful that no tyrant ever had forced me to grovel like that. No conversation about kneeling can begin without acknowledging how forced kneeling has been used as a form of subjugation.

And yet we should not allow our pain over the past to blind us to the meaning and power of kneeling as a spiritual response to awe. What is kneeling when it is not forced upon us by an autocrat? What might kneeling be as the natural response of a free being? Has there ever been an experience of awe so overwhelming to you that it took your breath away and brought you "to your knees"?

We may say we long for such moments. Yet for the most part we guard ourselves carefully against them. Loss of control is frightening, and we prefer to filter our experience to maintain our composure. We fear that which connects us to the unknown, to magnificence and majesty beyond our control. Yet in protecting ourselves, we become dulled; we lose a link to the sacred.

That the letters comprising the root of *brakha* and *breikha*, "blessing" and "fountain," also teach us *berekh*, "knee," is therefore a very powerful teaching. For *berekh* calls to us, "Do not shut down! Know awe! Live in reverence. Allow yourself to open and fill with the miracle of it all. In joy and trembling, kneel."

Medieval tales often tell of a king traveling among his people in disguise. He is in common garb among the throngs on the road or in the press of the crowd in the marketplace. Yet somehow people become aware of whose presence they are in. An electric hush takes hold as the wave of recognition travels. It is a magical moment. Everything was ordinary and then suddenly a veil is lifted. With a rush of comprehension everyone grasps that they are in the presence of the highest nobility . . . and they kneel.

I find in this response a compelling model for living our lives, aware that God is traveling incognito right beside us, awaiting our recognition. In those moments of recognition, we kneel and find splendor, majesty, and gentle wonder. As our ancestor Jacob exclaimed upon awakening from his vision of angels ascending and descending the ladder spanning heaven and earth, "God was in this place, and I, I did not know!" Like Jacob we are each invited to allow the Living Presence to take us by surprise and to awaken us to what has been there all along.

The word *berekh* requires the cultivation of awe and reverence, wonder and deep humility. These are essential attributes of any individual or community walking the path of blessing. But for many of us the word "humility" has been clotted with more undesirable than positive connotations. We more often seek empowerment than humility. After all, consider servants, slaves, and women—indoctrinated to be humble, to "know your place," to be content with "your lot." Masters are rarely told to be humble! When we hear "humility," we often hear "doormat," lack of self-respect, disempowerment, loss of dignity.

We live in a time when it is finally possible to identify and reject all forms of degradation. Yet the need to reject powerlessness can be so strong that it is hard to experience humility as empowerment. Humility is not degradation. Oppression generates degradation. Humility is fullness, abundance, and effortless compassion.

Humility is knowing oneself as integral to a larger whole, a shimmering thread in a great web. When I fully grasp that I am part of all that is, part of life, part of the mystery, walls of separation break down. My spirit opens, and my anxieties about my status and worth fade away. Instead of filling myself by owning things, exercising power, or practicing one-upmanship, I feel whole and complete; I am part of the dance of life and God, and I know that my soul, like each soul, has its particular role, which no other soul can fill.

I feel my true nature as a sacred being in a sacred universe; I recognize that you too are sacred. This recognition leads me to ask: What is your story? What is your soul's journey about? After all, Jewish tradition teaches that each soul comes into the world both to learn and to teach. It could be that you came to teach what I came to learn! I need you. The web is incomplete without you. You would not have been born if your part was not critical.

Knowing that we are all part of God is crucial if human beings are to come together in a just society. No one is expendable. No one is refuse.

Humility means that I fully comprehend and live in the bond of our connectedness. This realization offers me the extraordinary opportunity to find out, not how I can exploit you, but how all that our souls came to teach can inform one another's spiritual journey. In this way we grow together toward becoming a sacred community.

The Hebrew word usually translated as "humility" is *anavah*. Jewish teaching views *anavah* as one of the highest spiritual states. In the state of *anavah* one's most expanded consciousness and one's mundane consciousness are in harmonious attunement. In *anavah* we can each be an open channel, a conduit through which an exalted awareness of God can flow into our most ordinary and seemingly trivial actions.

Let me share with you a beautiful way in which a Hasidic master, the Maggid of Mezrich, framed this teaching. Rabbi Dov Baer, who was called the Maggid, the holy preacher, was a disciple of the Baal Shem Tov. One day, the Maggid heard the Baal Shem Tov expounding on the verse in Torah, "And the man Moshe [Moses], was more *anav* than any other human on the face of the earth." (Numbers 12:3) Listening to him, the Maggid wondered about the actual spiritual state being described by the word *anavah*.

He offers us an exquisitely crafted teaching. "There are two levels of awareness," he said. "One is when a person's consciousness is at the highest, most expansive state possible. Even when engaged in the most mundane matters, such a person is beyond crass material attachment. The second level, well . . . the person is not so removed." I truly enjoy the way the Maggid offers this opening observation with such compassion and lack of judgment. With great gentleness, he wants us to understand what we can aspire to, and yet not feel overly disheartened or bad about ourselves if we have not yet become all we can be.

The rabbi goes on, exploring the teaching further by recalling two special moments recorded in Torah. In the first, God wants Jacob to bring his family down into Egypt. God calls out: "Yaakov! . . . Yaakov!" The other occurs at the Burning Bush, where God calls out to Moses: "Moshe! . . . Moshe!" God calls each by name twice.

Now, although Torah is traditionally written without any punctuation, chanting the text conveys the punctuation. The Maggid observed something unusual: the cantillation markings call for a strong breaking pause between "Yaakov" and "Yaakov" and a purposeful, smooth vocal glide between "Moshe" and "Moshe." The teacher asks, "How should we understand this? Why the difference?"

The Maggid suggests a radical explanation. Torah wants to teach us about the two levels of consciousness at work within each person: our ordinary consciousness and our most expanded consciousness. God, the rabbi suggests, calls to each person twice to address both levels! Within Moshe there is "Moshe-of-most-expanded-consciousness" and "Moshe-of-ordinary-consciousness"; both levels exist in Yaakov as well. When God calls, God calls to both levels in each person. That is to say, God wants to reach us no matter what level we've attained. In the case of Moshe there is no dramatic pause because the two levels of his consciousness are attuned. The melody flows gracefully from "Moshe" to "Moshe" because God-awareness flows gracefully through Moshe, uniting his highest self and most mundane self in a single stream.

Moshe models the possibility that a person can sustain the most expanded consciousness even when occupied with mundane matters. This openness is the goal. Yaakov's call is melodically disjunctive while Moshe's is fluid because Moshe is, as Yaakov is not yet, a fully open channel; whether Moshe's task is exalted or ordinary, the most expansive awareness moves effortlessly through him.

When, the Maggid says, we achieve and sustain this openness to the presence of God, then we know true humility. This is *anavah.*

For Moshe, it was precisely because his link to the highest awareness never closed that "he never imagined himself of more personal significance than other people around him, even those whose
consciousness was the least evolved."

Anavah/humility enables the soul to be a true vessel of holiness. We can each experience moments of *anavah* when we apprehend that we are each an expression of God, and see every moment
as an opportunity to touch the divine glory. The cathedral of this
experience of holiness is not a building you go to; it is right inside
you, constructed by every moment of your life. We build it by let-
ting go of our need to manipulate, control, and judge so that we
may relearn how to simply be.

Years ago, my friends and I would ski on the slopes of a
country-club golf course on the outskirts of our Long Island
neighborhood. I was never quite brave enough for downhill skiing,
but I found these slopes offered an approximation of the "rush" I
imagined downhill skiing could be. I experienced a real thrill out
there on the snow. I could trudge up to the top and then let loose!
On my skinny cross-country skis I could sail down the cascade of
hills. I could flex my knees and it would feel as if I had become
part of the swell of the snowy earth beneath me. Somehow my
knees would adjust effortlessly to every rise and fall. For just a few
seconds of eternity, I rode the hills with supple grace. I felt like a
jockey who was not riding but had "become the horse." My "self"
disappeared into pure exhilaration. No past or future, only NOW!
An inexpressible aliveness flowed through me—a gift of God,
which I offered back into God. Sensations shifted and my body
adjusted effortlessly...until some part of me somehow noticed
that it was "working," that I was soaring, that "I" (hooray!) was

actually skiing! Yes! I was doing it! I was ... and, that very instant, crash! I'd fall.

Where did the "flow" go? I was in it and then it was gone! I was it and then suddenly I was observing it, evaluating it, outside of it. ... So there I was sitting in the snow again, realizing that here was a metaphor for living. Yes, I could ski, but only as long as I could let go of my "self." In order to be present I had to ease out of my ego's self-consciousness. I had to move beyond my pride or worries or fears and give myself over to becoming part of something larger than my "me." I had to be so fully in the skiing that I could let go of "me."

Frankly, it isn't all that easy to be fully present, receptive, and inside the moment. I'm more of a Yaakov than a Moshe most of the time. Oh yes, sometimes I'd fall because I just wasn't skilled enough to navigate a rough spot or because a branch would catch the skis. But far more often it was the consequence of an inner shift I recognized as the intrusion of my own self-consciousness. The holiness of the moment lies in remaining open and sensitive to every nuance of NOW, thus remaining in the *anavah!*

I remember realizing with a smile that it was the same for love-making as for skiing. Only when I allow myself to melt away can I give and receive in the intimate now. The holiest moment is now! God is present in this moment, now. Moshe may model the possibility of living fully in the now of God, but even for the Yaakov types among us moments of *anavah* can be known, held, and savored.

Rabbi Shlomo of Radomsk taught that only in the light of this realization can we truly understand Yaakov's exclamation: "God was in this place and I, I did not know!" According to Rabbi

Shlomo, Yaakov meant, "[I could see that] God is in this Place, [because at that moment, my] 'I' [my self-conscious ego] I did not know." Said the rabbi in Yaakov's voice: "If the Presence of the Holy One indeed dwells here, if I have invoked the holiness in this place, it must be because 'My I, I did not know.' Somehow I must have emptied myself of everything that clogged me, my sense of self-awareness, any consciousness of ego, any trace of self-intention, so that everything in me could now be only for the sake of the Holy Name."

When we know ourselves born of the fullness of God, holy vessels of God's holy light, we know beyond any ego-attachment the true nobility of our souls. How strange that true humility and true nobility are companions. *Berekh*/knee teaches us that we can achieve *anavah* and hold the God-awareness flooding through us. The result is an exultation and a great dignity neither degrading nor triumphalist. It is rather a luminous feeling, a profound and selfless grace.

Being an *Eved*, Serving with Love

To Me the Children of Israel are servants.
They are My servants whom I brought
out of the land of *Mitzrayim*/Egypt.
I am יהוה your God.

—LEVITICUS 25:55

These powerful words of Torah speak of the flight from Egypt, a miraculous liberation revealing our God as a liberating power, sup-

porter of the downtrodden and oppressed. Each spring at Passover
we gather to relive this time and sing the songs of our freedom:
"*Avadim hayyinu . . . va'ata b'ney chorin.* We were slaves and now we
are free!"

How strange to read then in Leviticus that the Holy One
seems not to mean us to be free. In freeing us from the servitude
of Egypt, God prepares us for another kind of service, as servants
of God. How shall we understand this?

The passage evokes a poem by the eleventh-century poet
Yehudah HaLevi:

Slaves of temporal powers, slaves of time,
they are slaves of slaves!
Only the *eved Adonay*, the servant of God,
alone is free.
Therefore, when each human being searches
for his portion of life,
chelki Adonay
my portion is God!
This is what my soul calls out:
"Let my portion be God!"

What then is an *eved Adonay*, a "servant of God," a servant who
is free?

In the desert of Sinai, our stories tell us, where the vast
parched wilderness stripped everything down to bare essentials, we
absorbed the voice of God with such intensity that we experienced
synesthesia: Our "ears saw and eyes heard." Legend tells us that
heaven and earth touched, revealing to Moshe the underlying pat-

terns of Creation. Perhaps there in the desert, with the gods of Egypt behind us, we came to understand that to serve the limited is to be truly enslaved. We began to discern that when we serve the Whole, everything temporary and partial loses its power over us. For then our hearts are already filled with everything we need. The power of external forces over us is diminished.

This is how I understand the many warnings in Torah against "idolatry." The Hebrew word usually translated "idol," *pesel*, is very interesting. The term "idol" conjures up a statue, but *pesel* does not actually mean "statue." Rather it refers to "something-that-is-less-than-the-whole." A Torah scroll missing letters because they have flaked off the parchment is called *pasul*, deficient, less-than-whole. We may not read from a scroll that is *pasul*. We may not take something partial and elevate it to the status of the whole.

As a people we learn to hear in the repeated warnings against idolatry the imperative, "Do not serve anything that is a *pesel*, that is *pasul*, less-than-the-whole! Serve only the One!" Perhaps we might frame the ancient Hebrew affirmation of God's unity in a contemporary idiom and say: *"Shema,* Wake up! Understand! The smallest patterns you can see are reflected on a cosmic scale in the patterns of the universe. Don't focus on a mere part imagining that it is the entirety."

A story is told of Rabbi Yosef Yitzhak Schneerson of Lubavitch who was arrested by the Communist secret police for teaching Torah in defiance of the authority of the State. During the interrogation, enraged by the rabbi's obstinate silence, the commander pulled out his pistol and put it to the great man's head. "This little toy has made many people talk," he sneered. "This is my 'convincer.' "

The rabbi's response shook me. Facing death, he replied, "You who serve many gods, and have only one life in which to serve, you the 'convincer' would convince. But I have only one God, and many lives in which to serve. Your 'convincer' does not convince me."

In that moment the authority of the police disappeared. The Rebbe did not serve them. He did not serve the convincer; he did not serve their power and he did not serve their state. The only thing that they could do to him, kill him, did not convince him, and so he remained a free man.

The role of the servant of God is not subjugation, but to be an extension of God in the world, an open channel. This is the freedom empowering Reverend Martin Luther King, Jr. to walk the walk of freedom, enabling Archbishop Oscar Romero and the liberation priests of Latin America to defend the poor and oppressed at risk of their own lives. No temporal power could take from them the truth of their purpose as servants of God, extensions of God's desire to uplift the oppressed.

Both King and Romero were murdered for their passionate persistence, but no ruler could bribe them, no money could buy them, no threat could move them. The call of the God of compassion and justice was the only compelling convincer. "Be my *avadim*, my servants," God calls to us. "Serve the Oneness of all Creation and be free."

"They are My servants whom I brought out of the land of *Mitzrayim*. I am יהוה your God." It is perhaps not by accident that the word for "Egypt," *Mitzrayim*, more literally means "narrowness" or "constriction." Its root letters *TzR* are related to the *TzR* in Hebrew *tzarot*, most familiar as the Yiddish word *tzuris*. In ordinary life, *tzuris* is what you have when you are late for your big-break job interview but you are speeding back home because you remember you left the stove on. Next your car's transmission breaks down and you hop a cab to your front door, only to realize that you've left your keys in your disabled car. As you watch the cab disappear round the corner, you experience *tzuris,* the pain of being squeezed.

Our people's liberation from Egypt was a historic liberation from bitter squeezing pain, the *tzuris* of *Mitzrayim.* We celebrate this liberation every year in the re-enactment around the Passover table. Even as we celebrate, we understand that the external "liberation from *Mitzrayim"* points us toward our inner spiritual liberation from narrowness and constriction—from the pain of being squeezed within lives and habits that suffocate our souls.

As ancient Hebrews we exchanged Egypt's "fleshpots" for a windswept desert where we will most potently hear the voice of the One Power. Each of us staggers out into freedom only to relearn how to serve. Witnesses to moments when we too feel heaven and earth touch, we each feel God's Presence, we "hear God's Torah" and begin to understand what it might mean to live daily with awe and love as our companions. We learn with growing humility and insight to cultivate soul-expanding attentiveness to the flow of blessing. Humility then becomes a quiet strength, a gentle radiant power we know does not belong to us.

In this process we discover that we cannot separate religion and world, cannot act as if "spirituality" were a personal pastime unrelated to global suffering and injustice. As our connection with God and our consciousness of the Whole expands, we comprehend that our own fullness cannot be achieved alone. The creative life of the spirit is stifled by injustice. Our very openness binds us to the joy and pain of others. We find the depth of our caring and compassion growing. Moshe was warned at Sinai that he could not absorb the full radiance of God's "face" and live, but he was privileged to know the divine essence: nurturing, compassionate, patient, abounding in kindness, extending love through thousands of generations, forgiving error. Jewish sages teach us: "Finite person, you can't be God, but you are in the pattern of God. Just as God is compassionate, YOU be compassionate. Just as God is loving, YOU be loving."

In Genesis we read that on the sixth "day," when the Creation of all that exists was complete, God surveyed all that had been made, and declared creation to be "very good." Very good—but not perfect. Jewish teaching offers us the wisdom that the world was left incomplete so that human beings might enter into partnership with God in the task of completing and perfecting. We are each called to be part of a great *tikkun*, a healing and repairing of Creation. This is our liberation and our service. Every *mitzvah* and every *brakha* proclaims our partnership in this ongoing work.

We are invited to reflect upon all of this when we say the word *barukh*.

אתה

Du, Du, Du!
You! You! You!
I want to sing a "You-Song" to You!
Du, Du, Du!
Where can I find You?
And where can I not find You?
Wherever I go: You! — Wherever I stay: You!
Only You! — None but You! — Again You!
Always You!
Du, Du, Du, Du!
When things go well: You! — God forbid, ill: You!
Ay, Du, Du, Du . . . Du, Du, Du!
Du, Du, Du . . . Du, Du, Du!
You! You! You!
East: You!   West: You!   North: You!   South: You!
You! You! You!
Skyward: You!   Earth: You!   Above: You!   Below: You!
Du, Du, Du . . . Du, Du, Du!
You! You! You!
Wherever I turn myself: You!
Wherever I remain: You!
Du!

—Rabbi Levi Yitzhak of Berdichev

ברוך **אתה** יהוה אלהנו מלך העולם

A Fountain of Blessings are **You**

Ata

❧✦❧

As we grow in our receptivity to awe and wonder, our souls expand, filling to overflowing from the Fountain. We kneel before that which fills all, surrounds and transcends all. Ever more open to the mystery, we find humility and hear the call to serve with joy. One might think this would be enough: to feel the Power, to open the self, stretching the soul to hold the joy and pain of a whole world. Yet our *brakha* has not ended, it has only just begun.

Even the wording of our *brakha* seems to urge us onward. If *barukh* has done its work well, we are ready for the next challenge. For me the next word of our *brakha* sometimes feels as though I am being asked to jump across an impossible chasm, and at other times being invited to slip, with a sigh of relief, into a warm bath.

What is happening? What does our *brakha* want of us now?

This further stretch is a very personal one, involving risk and trust. We are asked to step into an intimate dimension, to face the One Power as we would face someone very close to us. Our *brakha* asks us turn toward the Power we call God, not as "IT" but as *Ata* "YOU."

At times we may be filled with doubt and reluctance. This turning can seem like an unimaginable leap of faith. Still, we are asked to try. Our *brakha* is challenging us to open ourselves to the experience of intimacy: to enter tentatively, cautiously, hopefully, expectantly, and consciously into a personal relationship with God. We call out to God as You because You is personal. There was a time when God was invoked in English as "Thou," as by *du* in Yiddish or German, or *tu* in French, the most intimate form of address. Ironically, "thou" is now an archaic form, and sounds stiff to our ears. English no longer has a vernacular intimate pronoun; "you" must suffice.

We call out to God as "You" because this is the language of relationship. It is, after all, with the living "you"s in our lives that we practice relationship and learn all we know of intimacy. We long to know and be known, to love and be loved. While certainly the divine reveals itself to us when we stand in awe before the wonder and mystery of the universe, we just as often discover God in profoundly intimate moments we share with another, with a beloved, with children, with friends, or in coming to know our own innermost selves.

Even our experiences of God in nature are rooted in our humanity. "From my flesh I see God," says Job. All I know of God is filtered through my humanness. When I feel my relationship with God is one of intimacy, I know of no other language to express it than the language of human intimacy. In my relationship with God

I find all the feelings of hope, fear, and exaltation I find when I bare soul and self to my beloved. To tell my friends I love my life partner bears no comparison to the experience of saying *to* him, "I love YOU." To talk about divine energy is not nearly as hard as calling out to God as a living and conscious presence, a "You."

I recognize my caution, confusion, and doubt: a conscious power? A sentient universe? A personal relationship? Yet I know that beyond separateness lies another reality; only the language of relationship can take me there. And so I call out to the One and enter into a covenant of mutuality. I make a commitment to be present to that relationship.

Entering into relationship with God means finding God in our lives, opening ourselves to the presence of divinity all around us. God winks at us from everything, reminding us that beneath the surface appearance of things lies a deeper reality. Yet we most often do not see. Around us, most everything appears inert and separate. The underlying oneness is far from apparent. God is hidden.

Isaac Luria, the sixteenth-century master of Kabbalah called the *Ari*, "the Lion," describes the earliest moments of Creation when the Holy One, whose light filled the allness, contracted that one endless light, withdrawing Self into Self to make space into which Creation could issue forth. From this teaching we understand that for Creation to exist, God must withdraw and limit the full intensity of the divine light. To nurture existence divinity must self-conceal. It is through this self-diminution that the Infinite gives life to, supports, and cherishes the finite.

This concealing of the infinite grants us our existence as physical beings, and offers us "the illusion of our separate identity." In the ordinary world, most everything appears to be a separate "thing." This is where our mundane consciousness dwells. No matter how much I care about you, you are still a separate person from me. Our separateness is wonderful and also painful. Yet through self-transcending moments of intimacy we can strip away the illusion of separateness and "catch an authentic glimpse of true Oneness." Intimacy offers us the gift of easing past our aloneness, into our oneness. The oneness glimmers just beyond the veil of separateness which intimacy renders transparent. Perhaps we can say that we use an intimate and personal form of address for God to train ourselves to experience God shimmering through every relationship we have.

The much-admired modern Jewish teacher Rabbi Abraham Joshua Heschel taught that it is not because God has no face that Jews make no portraits of God. Rather, he said, the reason is that all faces are God's Face. To select one and elevate it above the others would be incomplete, deficient, *pasul*. Every time I say "you" to my beloved, I speak also to God. Every time I say "You" to God, I affirm the Presence of that You in every other you. I must see God in each face, in each *you*, or I risk treating you as a use-object, an "it."

Martin Buber, a Jewish philosopher of prewar Germany, tells of an experience that brought home to him the peril of turning an opportunity for true relationship into an encounter with an "it." It is said that Buber wrote his masterwork, *I and Thou*, because of this experience.

In my mind's eye I see Buber, great teacher of philosophy and practitioner of meditation, living in a house surrounded by a walled garden one enters through a wooden archway door. Inside, in the morning with the sun risen just enough to dance on the

herbs, Buber loved to meditate. On this occasion, after a morning
of religious enthusiasm, there was a disturbance, a rattling on the
latch of the wooden gate. In rushed an agitated student, a boy of
seventeen, awkward and uncomfortable, clearly wanting to ask
Buber something but unable to say it plainly. Buber, still in the
afterglow of meditation, responded disconnectedly to the questions and the boy left unheard. Later that day the boy ended his
own life. He had come to the great teacher for help at the last possible moment, but Buber had failed to recognize the boy's need.
The philosopher had objectified the boy, turned him into an "it."

The introspection brought on by Buber's grief is said to have
engendered "I-Thou," the passion for full relationship that became
Buber's lifelong spiritual project. He called the ability to be present
to the humanity and Godliness of another person (or even another
creature) "the life of dialogue." Here we see past what is superfi-
cial, into the essence. We emulate the eye of God and see into the
heart. When we enter into I-Thou relationship, we break through
our usual sense of detachment and separateness into true intimacy.
I bring my whole being to meet you. We extend ourselves to meet
each other and find ourselves being met, being known.

A beautiful I-Thou story is told of the rabbi of a small Jewish
village, a *shtetl*, in Eastern Europe. One Friday afternoon, a few
hours before sundown when Shabbos would begin, a man came
into his study with a question. "Rabbi," he asked, "is it permitted
to make *kiddush* [the sanctification blessing for Shabbos] over
milk?" "Hmmm," said the rabbi, thoughtfully shaking his head.
"No," he replied, "it is not. But what an interesting question. You
know, a strange thing happened this week. Early on Sunday, a
wealthy man stopped here and had a difficult question for me.

When he left, he gave me seven rubles and told me to award them to whoever brought me the most intriguing question during the remainder of the week. It is Friday afternoon, almost Shabbos, and the week is over. I think the seven rubles belong to you."

No sooner had the amazed man left with his seven rubles than in burst the rabbi's wife and several of his students. "Why," they demanded, "did you lie to him! Surely you know that, while it is preferable to make *kiddush* over wine, it is perfectly permissible to make *kiddush* over milk. And that story about the rich man! You made that up!" "Ah," said the rabbi. "What you say is true, but you are missing the point. In his question I heard his need. He had no money to buy wine, or even a chicken for his family's Shabbos. In his poverty he would have had to make his *kiddush* over milk. Now he will buy wine and food, and his Shabbos will be joyous."

Buber has said that "all real living is meeting." When we truly meet an other, we are fully present. We penetrate beneath appearances and can really hear, really understand. We touch the other's essence, and in so doing discover our own aliveness.

As we are to each other, so we are to God. The *Ata* of our *brakha* opens our I-Thou relationship with God. Says the *Zohar*, "All of Creation took place [because] the Holy One [desired to] be known and recognized by all creatures." Just as we long to be met, to be known, God too longs to be known. A *brakha* addresses God intimately, affirming that we know "You," for our awareness of You reflects our life as a part of You. We are "chips off the old block," born of Your desire to be known.

When we call out to our Source as "Thou," or "You," this small word internalizes the big faith that we can be met. Calling out to God as "Thou" does not caricature God as an oversize anthropomorphic deity in a distant heavenly abode. (In fact, the teaching that we are "in the image of God" is better understood to suggest, not that God is anthropomorphic, but that we are "theomorphic"—living reflections of the divine pattern, fractals of a larger consciousness.) We call out to God as "Thou" because we experience an awareness reflected back to us from the world, when we are willing to enter into relationship with it.

We, all life, and all that is, derive from a conscious urge toward self-expression fundamental to the universe, intimately part of us, even while utterly beyond us. While it has been common in science to describe consciousness as a rather mysterious product of the increasing structural complexity of life, our *brakha* asserts the opposite. Our *brakha* claims that awareness or consciousness is not an accidental product of the complexity of life but in fact the primary and ultimate reality. Consciousness, says the Thou of a *brakha*, not materiality, is the ground of being. Our consciousness derives from and mirrors a divine consciousness, the living Thou of the universe.

You have perhaps heard theologians speak of Creation as an act of divine "will." Yet the Hebrew word for "will," *ratzon*, can be better translated as "wanting" or "desire." Creation in all its abundance is the ever-present welling up of divine desire. We are the flowering into life of God's longing to be known. Our awareness is an expression of a divinity resident throughout Creation, one fulfillment of an immense cosmic process that attains fullness of expression in us. We are the children of divine self-expression. Our own desire and longing to be known is a reflection of the greater longing that births us.

With each *"Ata"* of a *brakha* we call out, "I am from You; I am of You. Do you recognize me? I am turning my face to You; do turn Your face to me." In our longing for intimacy, to know and be known by God, we turn to face God and call God to face us. The first words of praise of Jewish prayer sung upon arising every morning are, "I am grateful as I face You." We hear an echo of the ancient prayer of the *kohanim*, the priests of the Holy Temple, who blessed us saying, "May God's face shine upon you and bring you peace." We turn to face God and find God turning toward us.

Like lovers who begin by spotting each other across a room, we move closer to ever-fuller communion. "Love," observes the *Zohar*, "begins with physical attraction. Then lovers begin communication and speak. As they become closer they stop speaking and are aware of each other's breath. Finally, they become closer still, and their communication becomes a kiss. At this moment of the kiss they feel each other's life force.... The two mouths come closer and closer and progress from speech to breath to kiss. [These same] four stages of intimacy in love: physical attraction, speech, breath, and kiss, exist in the relationship of a person and the divine."

Thus, in Torah, Moshe is said to have known God *"panim el panim,* face to face." This is "the kiss," the ultimate "inter-face" in which we offer our own life-force into God and receive life from the Life Force itself.

In a *brakha* we call out to God as "You" and turn ourselves to face the Beloved. In our turning we arouse reciprocity. As I turn to face my beloved, my beloved turns toward me. *"Ani l'dodi v'dodi li,"* chants the singer of the Song of Songs. "I am my beloved's and my beloved is mine." Both turnings can, however cautiously

begun, become graceful and harmonious in time. Calling out to
God as "You" is the initiating gesture of that turning.

Hebrew, a Gendered Language

When we turn from the English "You" or "Thou" as our doorway
to the wealth of teaching on intimacy and the unity of God, and
engage with the Hebrew *Ata,* we encounter a gender "ouch." The
Ata form of "You" in Hebrew is a male form of address. Hebrew
has no neuter forms. Every noun/pronoun, is grammatically either
feminine or masculine. One cannot speak of, or to, anything or
anyone without using words indicating gender.

    While Jewish teaching may be clear that the You with whom
we converse when we call out to God includes and transcends all
gender, the traditional words of a *brakha* use the masculine form.
For many, this exclusively male language is distancing and painful.
It may seem easier to use English, which glides us past this
dilemma because "You" in English is not gender-specific. In
Hebrew, however, there is no end run around gender. What should
we do?

    Although Jewish tradition reminds us again and again that the
Endless One is beyond all duality, a true union of all seemingly
opposing forces, and therefore both entirely inclusive of and
utterly beyond all gender, the traditional language of prayer and
blessing offers mostly male words and images. Only in the mystical tradition do feminine images for God surface. But the mystical
writings have often been kept hidden from public view. Pushed

underground by many fears and pressures, including those of rationalist modernity, the mystical motifs have flowed like a hidden aquifer, silently irrigating the tradition from below but with little public acknowledgment. Jewish customs, ritual, liturgy, and holy days all have wells sunk deep into this underground stream but at the surface, in public prayer and observance, this is rarely made explicit.

With the destruction of most of the remaining centers of Jewish mystical teaching in Europe, the few surviving teachers and guardians of those aquifers of esoteric teaching became more reclusive than ever. Yet in the last few decades, in both America and Israel, there has been much well-digging. A concerted effort to locate and translate Jewish spiritual writings has offered us renewed access to Jewish imagery for the feminine aspect of God to help balance the dominant male vocabulary.

In Jewish Renewal and Jewish feminist circles there has been considerable experimentation with new ways of crafting prayer and blessings to include the feminine aspect of God along with the male. Understanding exclusive fixation upon male God language as a kind of idolatry, communities have begun to revisit the many traditional names for God in order to vary both the gender and the Name that is spoken.

As we begin to reclaim images of a more intimate God, names such as "Breath of Life" and "Life-Force of All the Worlds" have emerged. Some new blessings, such as those in Marcia Falk's pioneering work *A Book of Blessings,* seek to avoid either masculine or feminine forms of address by rephrasing the *brakha* to emphasize the "we" who bless: "Let us bless the Source of Life." It is not uncommon now to hear the traditional words of blessing used alongside or in combination with alternative names of God and feminine God-language. *Barukh Ata,* for instance, becomes *Brukha Aht* in the feminine. *Brukha aht Yah-Shekhinah* is one way to cast the opening phrase of a *brakha* in the feminine, blending the feminine form of the initial word with two names for the divine, *Yah* (as in *Hallelu-Yah*/Praise *Yah*) and *Shekhinah* (the feminine Presence of God).

The importance of the full inclusion of both male and female God imagery (and of both men and women in communal prayer) can be illustrated by juxtaposing the Hebrew words for man and woman, איש and אשה, *ish* and *isha.* The juxtaposition makes it apparent that each has a Hebrew letter the other lacks—the י of איש and the ה of אשה. These two letters taken together spell יה *Yah,* a form of God's Name, showing us that the fullness of God embraces male and female together equally.

It is doubly potent to see this lesson reappear in the Hebrew forms for "you." In antiquity, the feminine form of "you" was not את *aht* but אתי *ati.* This form, which appears in Torah, is vestigially present in modern Hebrew in other grammatical constructs. When we place the male form אתה *ata* next to the more ancient female form אתי *ati,* we see again how each word has a letter the other lacks, those same letters which when joined spell יה, God's Name.

The *Zohar* teaches us explicitly what these lessons illustrate: "Any place where the masculine and the feminine are not both present, God is not fully present." When we are drawn to seek "You," the quality we seek may at times "feel" male and at times female. "You are," says the *Tikkuney Zohar,* "the unity of all Your Names." There is only One You!

Yah, where shall I find You?
High and hidden is your Place;
And where shall I not find You?
Your Presence fills Time and Space.
I have sought Your nearness,
With all my heart I called You!
And going out to meet You,
I found You coming toward me.

—Yehudah HaLevi

∞

For the mind in harmony with the Tao
all selfishness disappears.
With not even a trace of self‑doubt,
you can trust the universe completely.
All at once you are free,
with nothing left to hold on to.
All is empty, brilliant,
perfect in its own being.
In the world of things as they are
there is no self, no non‑self.
If you want to describe its essence
the best you can say is Not‑two.
In this Not‑two, nothing is separate
and nothing in the world is excluded.
The enlightened of all times and places
have entered into this truth.

—Seng‑Ts'an

Naming God

There is a moment in Torah when, standing before the flames of the Burning Bush, Moshe seeks to know God's Name. "And when they ask me, 'What is His Name?' what shall I say to them?" Like the Moshe of Torah, the "Moshe" within me also stands before the Divine Presence, yearning to know God's Name. I call to God: "Like Moshe, I have spoken to You as 'You,' but how do I go further? We have begun to face each other, but despite my fears I want to be more fully open to Your Presence in my life. I long to call out Your Name as lovers do. But what Name can encompass You? Is there a Name through which I can know You? Are there some human syllables that could possibly define You?"

The Art of Naming

Before we can begin to explore the spiritual teachings informing
the quest to discern God's Name, we must take a closer look at a
peculiarly human activity: organizing our understanding of the
world through language.

What is naming?

Alone among living creatures, we humans understand the
world around us through the categories of experience which we
name. Perhaps we say there is a "sky" and it is "blue." These words
evoke commonly held images about which we hold an array of
shared assumptions. Most meanings associated with a word are
clusters of assumptions held in common by members of a culture.
If we change languages, the meaning of a common word sometimes changes significantly. What may seem a relatively simple concept in one language is in another culture's frame of reference
much more complex, or perhaps even entirely different in meaning.

The Hebrew word *shalom* provides a graphic example. It is one
of the most widely known Hebrew words. When I ask a group
what it means, invariably the responses are "hello," "goodbye," and
"peace." Now it doesn't take people long to realize that *shalom*
doesn't actually mean "hello" or "goodbye." The word serves those
functions because "peace" is a fine expression of both greeting and
hope for people's arrival or departure. What is more fascinating is
that *shalom* does not mean "peace" either, at least not with the same
nuance of meaning as it has in English.

The word "peace" enters English through the Latin *pax*. This
"pax" was a much-touted goal of the Roman Empire: the *Pax
Romana*, the "Roman Peace." But this was a peace achieved through

conquest. When all the "barbarian" rebel peoples who resisted being conquered and all the fit-only-to-be-colonized peoples were subdued, the Roman victory brought "peace." *Pax* means the extinguishing of conflict, the absence of hostility. This military derivation of the word "peace" is demonstrated by our agreement that the opposite of "peace" is "war."

The Hebrew word *shalom* bears astonishingly little resemblance to this "peace." As we have seen, in order to understand a Hebrew word we must look at the letters of its root, the three-letter core of consonants that is the word's source. In *SHaLoM* they are *SH-L-M*, or the Hebrew letters שלם *SHin Lamed Mem.* This root conveys the meanings of wholeness, completeness, fulfillment, and perfection.

The word *shalom* expresses the profound contentment we experience as inner peace. When I greet you with *"shalom"* I am not merely saying "hello" or "goodbye." I am offering you my hope and desire that you should experience the bliss of wholeness, fulfillment, completeness, and perfection, that you should know true inner peace.

Not surprisingly, the opposite of *shalom* is not war! More natural are words conveying a sense of lack-of-wholeness, fracturedness, and incompleteness, words like "alienation" or "exile." So, when I pray for *shalom* in the Middle East, I mean vastly more than the cessation of hostilities. I am naming a state of being and by voicing it hoping to call it forth.

Each act of naming brings us into relationship with the world. The words we use to name the world around us inform the way we understand what everything is and what it means. Every time I name, I define that relationship. I frame it with my concept.

Humans are born "programmed" with the latent capacity to name the world. Yet before we learn to draw any distinctions at all, much less name them, we have lived in the language-less blur of early infancy. Deep in our preverbal memory there lies the awareness of a time when we alone were all that existed. As newborn infants we experienced no difference between our "self" and the "world"; our sensations and feelings were all that existed. Just as to an infant the rattle in its grasp is not a rattle but a sensate part of its being, so it is with every sound, taste, and smell. A cry may bring a warm, sweet, satisfying sensation but it has no name. It is not separate from the infant me. I am not even aware of the separateness of my self because there is nothing against which it can be understood. There is only a flow of feeling.

Consciousness, emerging gradually, brings with it the awareness of patterns and distinctions. Gradually I become aware that there is a "Mama" who comes when I call. We are connected, but she is separate from "me." There is a "me" and there is "not me": Mama. She has a name. The world around me emerges with all its possibilities. There is so much, and everything has a name!

In a very real sense, as I name my world I call distinct realities into existence. I name and frame my world, creating order and assigning meaning. By naming I become in a way a co-creator of my world.

The explosion of awareness accompanying the acquisition of language is illustrated in a moving episode in the film *The Miracle Worker*. In this story a dedicated young teacher, Anne Sullivan, is engaged to teach the wild, undisciplined child Helen Keller, blind and deaf from very early childhood. With determined persistence, Anne presses sign-language onto Helen's palm but to no avail.

Locked incommunicado in a language-less darkness, the girl can't understand. Then one day at the yard fountain, Helen holds her hands under the rushing water as Anne signs into her hand the letters w-a-t-e-r, w-a-t-e-r. Suddenly a coarse sound emerges from Helen's throat, reverberating from her earliest childhood memories. She remembers a throat sound she had learned to make that corresponded to this sensation. Even though she can no longer hear her own voice, she cries out, "wa-wa! wa-wa! wa-wa!" Anne at once grabs Helen's hand and again signs w-a-t-e-r, w-a-t-e-r, as Helen calls out, "wa-wa! wa-wa! wa-wa!" In that epiphany, Helen opens to a new quality of consciousness. Everything has a name! She need not be locked into the solitary confinement of her darkness. As she runs madly from object to object learning name after name, worlds of possibilities are born.

When we name our world, we create opportunities to enter into relationship with what we have named. It is for this reason that the sharing of names is the first step in an introduction: "Hello, my name is . . ." By naming we wrap our minds around concepts and experiences, and describe them in a way that makes them comprehensible, retrievable, and manageable.

This sense of the awesome power of naming is perhaps even more clear in Hebrew than in English. Because English is a composite language with vocabulary drawn from many linguistic sources, we English speakers often think of naming as simply the assignment of a label, as a convention. We agree that this is "table"; we all use that word and this "is" a table. The sound-combination itself has no meaning.

Hebrew, however, because of its long history as a sacred language, embodies a radically different view. It is not only (as we have seen with *shalom*) that each word conveys meanings not necessarily similar to their conventional English counterparts. In Hebrew, words and names are not experienced as humanly assigned labels. A thing's "name" is understood to be an intrinsic expression of its spiritual essence. As we have seen, this teaching is embedded in the story of Creation in which the Holy One "speaks" Creation into being. All the material and spiritual energies constituting the totality of Creation are born by being called. Each element of Creation comes into being at the instant its "name" is expressed by that Power transforming its own singular energy into abundant manifestations of energy and matter.

Of course, it is difficult for translations of Torah to convey this complexity adequately. For instance, the most common translation of Genesis 1:3—"Let there be light"—seriously understates the terse, active, and expressive quality of the Hebrew, "*Yehi Or.*" *Yehi Or* conveys the sense of Creative Power actively calling out the energies bursting forth as radiance, both physical and spiritual. An imperative voice, "Light! Exist!" comes closer. More descriptive of the process, although hardly felicitous in English, might be: "And God expressed, 'All letter energies combining to manifest physical and spiritual Light: Be!' "

Jewish teaching treats Hebrew letters and syllables as the sound/energy articulations of the Divine ex-pression. They are constituent spiritual-physical energies of Creation, combining to form the substance of all existence. Calling out the "syllables" expressing the spiritual essence of each thing brings that thing into being. Language is therefore foundational to existence, not subsequent to it. The true name of an object or a creature is its innermost essence, a map of its energetic structure. A true name is therefore not an arbitrary label, a mere convention, but the vocalization of a fundamental essence we have discerned.

One of the ways we are created in the divine image is that with our utterances we too create worlds of meaning. In using language, we carve out meaning from chaos; we invoke our power as co-creators. This is why in Torah we read that the first assignment given to the newly created first human is to name the other creatures.

It is only when we grasp the depth of the concept of naming that the *Adam*'s task becomes truly clear. Newly created, unarmored, the androgynous human is alive and open to all the energies of Creation. For the *Adam* just to be in the presence of a thing is to know it fully, to grasp the totality of its essence, to feel the immanent power of divinity calling it into being. But although God cannot speak with vocal cords, the human being can. As each creature places its essence before the *Adam*, the *Adam* articulates as language the syllables of Creation energy forming its being. In an act of ultimate aliveness to the living presence of the divine-desire-to-create pulsing through each being, the co-creative partner of God calls out each creature's name.

What Is God's Name?

What is my name?
What is your name?
What is God's Name?
Our name is:
that we must be born

And the Creator's Name is:
to bear.
The soul alone
among all creatures
is generative
like God is.

—MEISTER ECKHART

If to name is to take a journey-into-essence, how could we imagine knowing the Name of God? The *Tikkuney Zohar* reminds us, "*Leyt machshavah t'fisah bakh klal,*" "No thought at all can grasp God." To name is to define and also therefore to confine, to limit. How can we describe the Essence transcending all essence? Naming is an act of calling-into-being. Can we call God into being?

⸻❦⸻

The crystal hanging in my window keeps its rear facets from me when the front faces me. It would not dance its colors across my kitchen were that not the case. I twirl it around but the only reason it refracts the light as wondrously as it does is that at every moment it always has a part which is hidden from my sight. It has an internal life and the light comes through it in a miraculous way. I can learn about the facets not facing me by looking at the ones that do. My hope is that the crystal will keep twirling so I don't wind up with only one facet facing me for too long. I don't want to see the facet as the whole. I don't want to imagine the facet is the crystal.

A disadvantage of language is that precise terms encourage our fixation on one small facet of an experience. It is easy to lose the whole and become attached to one limited aspect of an experience that is far more rich, varied, and complex than our focus. How often we use language to pigeonhole! We name something and think we understand it. We have it nailed down, boxed. We assign names to powers we can barely comprehend and imagine with false comfort that we have a handle on them. Naming can twist the truth. Getting stuck on a name, we can deny part of the truth.

By seeking to learn God's Name we may be attempting to appropriate God, to make God manageable, neat enough, packaged enough. Then just as comfortably as we can say, "This is my table," we might say, "This is my God."

The word "God" itself may exacerbate the problem. This word may convey a limited and static image. In English, the word "God," coming through Germanic origins into Old English, once meant "the invoked." Long divorced from this original meaning, the word has for too many become a caricature, evoking the image of a stern, bearded man on a throne.

In the context of the Hebrew sources, and despite the problem of gender, this anthropomorphic image and even the concept of "throne" are rich in possibilities for understanding particular facets of the crystal. However, detached from the richness of those sources and presented as the defining image, the enthroned male "God" offers a constricted and painfully limited picture. Rather than expanding our consciousness and deepening our connection experientially, this "God" may have the opposite effect.

A noble thinker once challenged Buber: "How can you bring yourself to say 'God' time after time? How can you expect that your readers will take the word in the sense in which you wish it to be taken? What you mean by the name of God is something beyond all human grasp and comprehension, but in speaking about it you have lowered it to human conceptualization. What word in human speech is so misused, so defiled, so desecrated as this! All the innocent blood that has been shed for it has robbed it of its radiance. All the injustice that it has been used to cover has effaced its features. When I hear the highest called 'God,' it sometimes seems almost blasphemous."

Full comprehension of the essence of the divine, at each moment calling us and the universe into existence, may be beyond the grasp of any finite being. Yet something of God's power is alive within and around us. My soul in love and longing, in terror and trepidation, opens to the power in English called God. But "God" is not God's Name.

At best, "God" (like president) is a job description, far better used as a verb than as a noun. "God" is a word we become attached to, imagining that the word itself defines God's essence. Often, when I write, I employ a Jewish custom of placing a disconcerting dash "G-d"—into the word God. This custom induces a perceptual jolt, reminding me that "God" is not God's Name or essence but only a pointer.

Throughout Jewish history we have used many "names" to describe our varied experiences of God moving in our many-faceted world. Yet always we sought a Name to unite and subsume all other names. Could there be a name evoking its own beyond-ness, a name in its very mystery echoing the Mystery? Perhaps in our deepest meditation, in our highest and most profound moments of awareness, we might be privileged to hear a name seeming to be an echo of such a Name.

Torah teaches that when God called Moshe to go back to Pharaoh to free the enslaved Israelites, Moshe questioned God: "If I say that God sent me and they ask me 'What is His name?' what shall I say to them?" The answer he heard was, *"Ehyeh Asher Ehyeh"*—usually translated "I will be what I will be." But I read this enigmatic phrase in varied ways: "I am Existence unfolding," or "I am Beingness becoming," or "I am the Eternal Am-ness," or even (drawing more closely on the specific energies of the Hebrew letters themselves) "I am the Oneness that lives and points toward life."

But what do these names mean? What is existence unfolding? What is eternal becoming? We know nothing of existence unframed by physicality. We are alive, but we do not even know what life is. We live immersed in time and yet do not know what time is. Finite beings, we live on the precipice of many mysteries. We may sense a Power moving beyond, within, and even prior to Creation, but as creatures of the physical world how can we even speak of this? A time before Creation? The moment of Creation originated time! Before Creation there was no "before." Of course, there was also no "there," for space also did not exist.

Before there was a before or a there, Oneness filled and did not fill non-time and non-space; there was neither filling of space nor passage of time. This is quite a mind stretch! We struggle to use our limited words to paint the dreamscape of an eternity of being, every non-moment enveloping time and space in an eternal now.

An eternal now uniting and transcending was-ness, is-ness, and will-be-ness? Our minds still cannot encompass this. We who live in a world of dimensionality do not function that way. *Leyt machshavah t'fisah bakh klal.* "No thought at all can grasp God!"

And yet in Torah the Holy One gives us a whisper. Moshe hears: "I am the Eternal Being. I am Being calling Being into Being each moment." Here is a glimpse of the divine essence as "existence itself." Through this hint we begin to learn a Name that is not a name, a Name transcending names, a Name including and subsuming all names.

יהוה

Now the moment I flowed out from the Creator
all creatures stood up and shouted:
"Behold, here is God!"

They were correct.
For you ask me: Who is God? What is God?
I reply: Isness.
Isness is God.

Where there is isness, there God is.
Creation is the giving of isness from God.
And that is why
God becomes
where any creature expresses God.

—MEISTER ECKHART

ברוך אתה יהוה אלהנו מלך העולם

A Fountain of Blessings are You, whose Name is יהוה

The Name Beyond Name

❧

This glimpse of the divine essence as existence itself leads us to look more closely at how Hebrew fashions the words for existence. When we look at the Hebrew verb of being, we see verb forms for "was": היה *hayah;* "is": הוה *hoveh;* "will be": יהיה *yihyeh.*

Recall that Moshe heard *"Ehyeh Asher Ehyeh"*—"I am Eternal Being, Eternally Becoming." Eternal being coalesces past, present, and future in a unitive now. Eternal being encompasses is-ness, was-ness, and will-be-ness, but is in itself none of these words. Or is it all of them? If we could somehow conflate "is," "was," and "will be" into one word, an "iswaswillbe," perhaps we would be closer to expressing the "power of eternal becoming."

Try this experiment, offered not to prove anything but to open a channel of insight. Spell out the Hebrew words for "is," "was," and "will be," and stack them up as if you're adding them together:

was-ness	*hayah*	ה י ה
is-ness	*hoveh*	ה ו ה
will-be-ness	*yihyeh*	<u>י ה י ה</u>
		י ה ו ה

From the first column starting on the right extract the lone י *yod* and bring it down below the line. In the next column we have the letter ה *hey* three times, and so ה is what we bring down below the line. The next column has two י *yods* and one ו *waw* (the more ancient pronunciation, now commonly pronounced *vav*). Place the two *yods* on top of the *waw* so that they disappear into the top of the *waw;* the three letters then visually meld together into a *waw* below the line. The last column again has three *heys,* and so we once more place a *hey* below the line.

We have now conflated "is," "was," and "will be" into four letters:

$$\text{יהוה} = \text{יהיה} + \text{הוה} + \text{היה}$$

"Iswaswillbe" becomes יהוה. It is this conflation of all the tenses of the verb "to be"—present, past, future—that constitutes in Hebrew the Divine Name.

Now, "iswaswillbe" is not exactly a word in English, but at least we can say it. The corresponding sounds for the Hebrew letters are Y, H, W, H. In Hebrew, however, as some of you may recall, letters are not necessarily accompanied by vowels. Vowels are not letters and need not be present. In any given word, vowels are assigned according to grammatical rules. But with a conflation, such as we have here, that represents no known part of speech, no vowels can be assigned to it!

This vowel-less nonword conveys a mind-stretching spiritual teaching. If you try to pronounce the sound these letters make (with no vowels), what happens? Try it. Y . . . H . . . W . . . H . . . You may discover that you cannot "say" any sound at all. You produce—what? Only an exhalation of breath! And then of course . . . you inhale!

Moshe's encounter with God led him to understand that God's Name lies hidden in the mystery of existence, in the "coming into being of the eternal now." In that Name, "is," "was," and "will be" merge as eternal existence, bringing together *yod, hey, waw* and *hey* in an unpronounceable breath. Thus every breath is the Divine Name! Every time we breathe, we breathe the Name of God.

The English language also knows this relationship between breath and the divine. The word "spirit" derives from the Latin verb *spirare*, "to breathe," perhaps related to the Hebrew *ruach*, meaning "breath," "wind" or "spirit." To "in-spire" is "to take in breath/spirit." So too at the end of life, we release our spirit, exhale one last time and "ex-pire."

Genesis teaches that the Holy One made the *Adam* from the *adamah*, the earth. God breathed into the lifeless *Adam*-earthling's nostrils the breath-of-life and the human being became a living soul. Breathing connects us to our source, to the Power "breathing" all creation into existence. God breathes life and soul into us by breathing into us God's own divine essence, God's own Name. Like lovers in the rapture of a kiss, sharing breath, sharing essence, God breathes spirit into us. We breathe deeply and are inspired!

You may be aware of a Jewish teaching "prohibiting" us from

pronouncing the name of God. It is true that we cannot pronounce the name of God! But "cannot" does not only mean forbidden; it also means it is simply not possible in any ordinary way. One way to understand this is that the Holy One revealed to us an unpronounceable name, thwarting our temptation to appropriate God. Just at the point where our use of language to define, limit, and control might be activated, Jewish tradition has inserted a profoundly counteractive experience. If we try to speak a limiting and confining name, we experience just the opposite: We try to pronounce the Name . . . and we breathe! Then we understand that the Name of God is neither Yahweh nor Jehovah; it is the breathing of soul and life energy into existence.

As we breathe, we remember not only that we cannot define and control the source of life but that the source of life unites us in a chain of reciprocity. My breathing out is your breathing in. The very molecules that were a part of me become a part of you. Breathing in oxygen, I exhale the carbon dioxide everything green "breathes" in to make more oxygen. Each breath revitalizes. With each breath we call God's Name and are inspired. Each breath is life.

It probably will not surprise you that the letter ה *hey*, the dominant letter of the Name, is the letter-energy of life force. With each breath we once again sing with the psalmist, *"Kol ha'neshama t'hallel Yah!"* "Every soul-breath praises God, the breath of life!"

The whole planet and the entire universe breathe the Name. We learn from physicists that ripples of Creation energy still flow from the original Great Flare, moving in a breathing motion as they dance in and out, expanding and contracting. We can sense not only our planet breathing the divine Name but all of Creation, expanding and contracting, breathing the symphony of the divine presence. The Name unites us all in a wondrous dance of being.

And so we have discerned that one way to know God's Name is by linking our own life-breath with the life-breath of Creation. Consider how it will affect even our casual conversation when we realize that each time we breathe, we call God's Name. Whenever we breathe we invoke the sacred. How this awareness will change the way we use our breath and our speech!

The Name uniting the many facets of the crystal, the Name calling us most fully to embrace the divinity breathing throughout Creation, is the one Name we cannot appropriate, the one Name we cannot own.

א

I have put duality away,
I have seen the two worlds are One;
One I see, One I know
One I see, One I call.

—RUMI

Says Isaiah: "Peace to the one who is far
and peace to the one who is near."
For one whose soul is in balance
realizes that s/he is far from God,
yet at the same time knows that s/he is near to God.
[We feel] trembling awe when we think of God as utterly
beyond. But from the sense that God is close,
love arises.

—RABBI LEVI YITZHAK

Aleph

⤜⤚

יהוה and א: Unity and Infinity

*S*hema Yisrael יהוה *Eloheynu,* יהוה *Echad!* Hear and comprehend *Yisrael,* You who wrestle with God, יהוה is our God, יהוה is One!

The central act of witness within Jewish prayer, the *Shema,* proclaims that the Name יהוה uniting, transcending, and subsuming all of being is One, the ultimate Oneness: All there is. We are asked to *"shema,"* to hear with total comprehension, to understand with complete awareness, that the Holy One is "Wholly One"—a singular power uniting and infusing all we are, and all we are a part of.

Yet Jewish wisdom on this subject does not end here. Recall that in the chapter introducing *barukh* we began to tell the story of God and Creation through the letters beginning with *aleph.* There we traveled deep within the infinite *aleph*-oneness of God, from which existence, with all its astounding variety, is born.

יהוה is infinite and one. *Aleph* is infinite and one. Perhaps the letter *aleph* itself can reveal to us further insight into the infinite unity we call God.

Each letter of the Hebrew *aleph-beyt,* as you know, is also a number. The letter *aleph* is both the first letter and the first number, the number one. There are no zeroes in Hebrew; non-modern texts did not use numerals. How could you indicate a thousand in Hebrew without zeroes? One way is by printing the *aleph* larger:

$$\aleph = 1 \qquad \aleph = 1000$$

To say, "a thousand," you pronounce *aleph* as *eleph,* altering only one vowel sound. To indicate a million, you could use an even larger *aleph.*

How might one symbolize infinity in this system? How big would the *aleph* have to be? After all, infinity is the ultimate oneness. There is nothing beyond infinity. The *Shema* calls us to affirm and witness God's infinite unity: "Comprehend! God is One: infinite, all-embracing, all that is. יהוה is א!"

If *aleph* is a way of representing the unitive infinity of God, then *aleph* must carry exceptional insights into the nature of that unity.

Look more closely at a very basic *aleph,* not calligraphically enhanced; we see something unusual. The single letter *aleph* א is itself made of three Hebrew letters. The two curved strokes on either side of the diagonal center line are each the letter *yod,* and the center line is a ו *waw (vav).* Recall that in Hebrew each letter's name is also a word. *Yod* means "pointing hand." *Waw* is a "hook," a conjoining and connecting letter which as a part of speech means "and." The oneness of *aleph* can be drawn as two hands, one pointing up and the other pointing down—or, perhaps, one pointing from the inside out, the other pointing from the outside in connected by "and."

One way of picturing this is:

The *yods*, one pointing toward us from beyond and one reaching upward and outward from within, bring to mind Michelangelo's ceiling of the Sistine Chapel, where the pointing hand of God reaches toward the outstretched hand of *Adam*. Sometimes, I too feel like *Adam*, that earthling, beckoned by the hand of God.

There are transcendent moments in each of our lives, however rare and exquisite, when we feel the infinite reach toward us, not from a familiar place within but from the Place beyond place.

Perhaps we stand at midnight on a hilltop, gazing out onto galaxies beyond number, facing a universe of dimensions beyond comprehension, and are carried up into the immense beyond-ness of it all. Somehow, from this vastness we feel addressed. Suddenly, we comprehend ourselves as part of a greater sentience calling us to our highest possibilities. Our smallness in the cosmic scale does not matter. We reach out to touch the heart of the universe and know we are sparks of a living source.

So too, there are times when we feel addressed, and the source is not beyond but seems very close, beside us, even inside us. With tenderness we look into the eyes of our child and we feel God's Presence dwelling right there. We see each other and know the Presence is immanent—alive in us and everywhere around us!

In the *aleph*, this is the other *yod* hand, reaching up toward us from the inside.

When we affirm that the Breath of Life of all Being, the Holy Name, is One, we unify the whole of our experience of God. The "out there" and "in here" meet.

Both the transcendent and the immanent dimensions of God call us. Jewish tradition asks us to be open to both the voice without and the voice within, listening to find the Place where they become one.

Over the course of our people's history, we came more and more to hear the voice within, the in-dwelling aspect of God, as a feminine voice. We called Her name *Shekhinah*, from the Hebrew verb *ShaKhaN*, to dwell. Always with us, *Shekhinah* is the Divine Presence infusing all of life. Hers is the intimate presence, stranger to neither our pain nor our sorrows, who feels most profoundly the torment of our exile and alienation.

When the Temple still stood in Jerusalem, it was our people's experience that *Shekhinah*-energy was felt most powerfully in the deep "within-ness" of the Temple's Holy of Holies. Perhaps we felt the energy meridians of the planet crossing at this sacred junction, like a God-magnet attracting the Divine Presence to concentrate within a most holy place. There for centuries we brought our songs, our prayers, and our offerings.

After the destruction of the Temple our teachers reminded us that the heart too is built of many chambers, with the Divine Presence dwelling there. Perhaps the external Temple was all along a "template" for what is already within us. Said the Chernobyler Rebbe, "Just as the Holy One condensed and concentrated the

Shekhinah into the Holy Ark of the collective Temple (as if the heavens of the heavens could encompass the Divine Presence!)...so too is the *Shekhinah* present in the individual temple which is the human heart." Each heart is an inner temple where the *Shekhinah* can always be found.

Creation cradles a balance of forces like the yin and yang of Eastern traditions. The *Shekhinah* hand of the *aleph* points upward from within. The downward-pointing hand beckons from beyond. The receptive in-dwelling Presence we began to encounter as the divine "feminine," the yin, is balanced by an outer, expressive, and projective energy we came to describe as the divine "masculine," the yang, often referred to as the *Kadosh Barukh Hu*, The Holy-One-Blessed-Be-He.

Says the Baal Shem Tov: "The Holy One Blessed Be He refers to the godly essence that is hidden from Creation. The Divine Presence/*Shekhinah*, on the other hand, refers to the godly essence that dwells in the physical world."

Sometimes we feel the beyondness hand of the *Kadosh Barukh Hu* reach toward us to hurl our lives in new directions: "You! Hello! Rosa! Refuse to sit in the back of this bus you are boarding." Or: "You! Hello! Look across the room right now. There is someone you must meet." Or: "Take that shortcut, the one that will cost you an extra five hours' drive. It is necessary that you be delayed." Sometimes this hand seems to call us against our will. "You want me to do what? To go where?" Often, we want to say, with Moshe: "Me? Pick someone else!"

The *Kadosh Barukh Hu* voice, penetrating our lives like a pointing hand from beyond knowing, calls us to exalt ourselves, to rise to the highest. The *Shekhinah* Presence within, shining with our joy and weeping with our sorrow, yet always present wherever we go, calls us to feel deeply and find divinity everywhere, radiant within us and around us.

The Oneness transcends and subsumes the essential qualities of both: projection and receptivity, expression and in-gathering. As creatures in the divine image, both the yin and the yang of God are within each of us. Just as we learned to feel the *Shekhinah's* presence within us, the *Kadosh Barukh Hu* is also within us. We are asked, therefore, to be nothing less than whole ourselves, to deny no aspect of our being. Men are not to deny their divine feminine nor women their divine masculine. Uniting both sides of our nature, we contribute to the healing by which alienation and exile are repaired and through which redemption comes into the world.

Shema Yisrael יהוה *Eloheynu* יהוה *Echad!*

Hear and comprehend *Yisrael,* You who wrestle with God,

יהוה is our God, יהוה is One!

אדני

When [Rabbi] Barukh came to those
words in the Psalm which read:
"I will not give sleep to my eyes,
nor slumber to my eyelids
until I find a place for the Lord,"
he stopped and said to himself:
"until I find myself and
make myself a place
to be ready
for the descending of the *Shekhinah.*"

—RABBI BARUKH OF MEZBIZH,
AS TOLD BY MARTIN BUBER, IN *TALES OF THE HASIDIM*

בדוך אחה יהוה אלהנו מלך העולם

*A Fountain of Blessings are You, whose Name is **Adonay***

Adonay

❧❧❧

יהוה ... this is My Name forever (לעלם *l'Olam*);
and this is my memorial *(zeh zichri)*
throughout all generations.

—Exodus 3:15

י׳הוה: This is my Name *l'Olam:* The word לעלם *l'Olam* [commonly translated "forever"] is written in this verse of Torah without the customary vowel-letter ו *waw* [making stark the root meaning: "to hide" or "conceal"; because of this omission, it is perfectly correct to read the verse as יהוה—this is my *hidden* name ...]

Torah is telling us that we must conceal the reading of the Name י׳הוה ... and not pronounce it.

On the other hand ... *zeh zichri:* The words *zeh zichri,* "this is my memorial," refer [not to to the Name יהוה, but rather] to the name *Adonay* ... Thus the sages have stated: "I am written יהוה, but I am pronounced *Adonay.*"

—Yosef Gikatilla

97

What Is in a Name

I love him.
I love you!
I love you, Yankel!

I know that sometimes, when we're not together, my big-hearted husband, Jack, daydreams a bit and thinks about me. It is something that I really love about him. Sometimes he even mentions me to somebody he's with, just to have the pleasure of feeling closer to me by talking about me. "You really love her, don't you?" a friend once commented to him. "Yeah," said Jack, "I do."

We both work at home, so sometimes in the midst of the onslaught of phone calls, the piles of bills and mail, the pressing schedule and urgency of coming appointments, we'll both stop. Our eyes meet. One of us says, "I love you."

If we're lucky, we'll have a bit of evening time together. We snuggle with Aaron, who is now seven-and-a-half, tuck him in, and sing the *Shema* and the angel song. With a tender sleepy smile, Aaron will pat me and whisper, "I love you, Mommy." My heart melts.

"I love you, Mommy." I float in that delight. Later, I turn to Jack, "I love you, Yankel." That's Yiddish for "Jack." I want him to hear "I love you" with his name. I realize that I too want to hear "I love you, Marcia" with my name. Not that "I love you" isn't great by itself, but "I love you, Marcia" breaks open my heart.

"I love her." "I love you." "I love you . . . Marcia." Each expression subsumes but surpasses the one preceding. If speaking *to* rather than only *about* one we love engages us more fully, we take a further step by calling her or him by name: "I love you, Yankel."

And so the Talmud teaches that merely to praise God is not a sufficient *brakha*. To be truly complete, a *brakha* should also address God by name.

The story is told in the Talmud of a shepherd, Benjamin, who said as a blessing for his meal, *Brikh marey d'hai pita.* "A Fountain of Blessings is the master of this bread." The question was posed, was that sufficient? Who is the master of the bread? When we enter into relationship, we do so with a "thou": Shouldn't we name the Thou to whom we speak? To have said a true *brakha*, the teachers concluded, Benjamin should have said, *Brikh Rachamana marey d'hai pita*, naming God as *Rachamana*, the Compassionate One, generous source of the life-giving bread.

Jewish wisdom teaches us an unpronounceable Name to remind us that the eternal power, the source of all, is beyond our appropriation. This is the "hidden" Name, hidden in its very unpronounceability; hidden because we can intend it but not say it, hidden because its very nature is to point beyond itself to the ultimate mystery of existence. When we see the Name, we can only pause and breathe.

The Name is mysterious and unpronounceable. So how are we to speak God's Name? When we really need to say something, what should we say? It is a powerful practice to hold God's Name in mind and breathe. But sometimes we really do wish to communicate and with intention call out to God by a name we can speak.

The naming of God reflects the multiple facets of the crystal revealed to our people. In Jewish (as in Islamic) tradition, we call the One by many descriptive Names. Jewish prayer is a rich treasury of God-names and words of praise. *Yotzeyr* means to create like an artisan from what already exists. We at times call God the great *Yotzeyr,* the "Artisan." We also call God *Borey,* the one who creates everything out of nothingness. We call God *Ha'Rachaman,* Source of Compassionate Love. *Rechem* means "womb" and *Ha'Rachaman* is the aspect of the Holy One we know as the Source of unconditional nurturance. We call God *M'kor Ha'Chayyim,* Source of Life; *Ayn Sof,* the Limitless, Without End; *Chey Ha'Olamim,* Life Force of Time and Space; *El Elyon,* the Most High; *Ma'ayan Raz,* The Mysterious Well; *Goel,* Saving Power; *Atika Kadisha,* the Ancient Holy One; *Yah,* Breath of Life; *El Ro'i,* God Who Sees Me; *Ha'Makom,* the Place of the World or the Place we go to. Sometimes we just call God *Ha'Shem,* The Name.

When we see the unpronounceable Divine Name in print or wish to allude to it in speech, it is customary to splice in another name, one of the various gateway names through which we direct our focused intention, our *kavvanah,* toward the One. There are many names, like *Rachamana,* chosen because of the particular experience of God which they evoke. Since the destruction of the Temple, however, the predominant custom in prayer, study, and blessing has been to hold the unpronounceable Name in conscious meditative focus while vocally substituting the name *Adonay.*

In most prayerbooks, *Adonay* is translated as "Lord." It is true that on the most pedestrian level *adon* is translated "mister" or "master." "Lord" is a synonym of "master" and has become another source of confusion and theological distress. When we hear "master," our conditioned impulse is to think of master/slave or master/servant. The word "master" connotes ruler, even oppressor, a meaning that

"Lord" reinforces. If God is my master, I am God's servant or slave; if God is my Lord, I am God's vassal.

As we have seen, to be a true *eved*, serving the Highest with pure *anavah*, is an exceptional spiritual achievement. However, in a contemporary milieu informed by a feminist critique and a striving toward egalitarian social ideals, *Adonay* as "Lord and Master" fails. The word not only feels like a capitulation to hierarchy but also seems to remind us that the divine hierarchy of power is male. Yet because of the import and uniqueness of this name and precisely because it has engendered so much discomfort, I have begun to explore what Jewish wisdom can teach us about this particular opportunity to experience God.

I propose deepening the discussion of *Adonay*. Jewish tradition teaches that each name we have for God-that-is-Beyond-Name is a point of access into a different relational experience with the One. Yosef Gikatilla, a thirteenth-century Kabbalist, wrote: "There are so many gates in the House of the One. Gates within gates! . . . They all are contained within the four-letter Name that is יהוה of Blessing. But each [gate] has [a unique Name] and function. Like a vast treasure-house with numerous chambers and a unique treasure within each one."

In a multifaceted crystal, each facet offers both a window and a refraction. Each face transmits only its unique refracted ray of the crystal's inner light out toward us. Our individual and collective experiences of God are not dissimilar. As we move in our own personal lives, so much changes. We go through so many emotional shifts, even in a single day. And as our collective journey unfolds, we as the Jewish people also change, adapt, flex, shift awareness. So too does our experience of God. As we move, the "crystal" moves. Different faces of the One turn to us as we turn different faces of our selves to the One.

Through the long history of our people's quest, we have learned to name these opportunities as we have experienced them. We have developed a rich and complex spiritual vocabulary. Each name offers an opportunity to encounter a particular quality of relationship with God. Each name is a gateway, a "chamber in the House of the One." The name *Adonay* is such a chamber.

What is *Adonay*?

Adon as Master

Rather than "turning us off," translating *Adon* as "master" can invite us to look more deeply at the experience of mastery. If we move beyond the master/servant motif, we encounter mastery in another sense, that of the "master craftsman," one who has perfected an art or skill.

Perhaps you have an endeavor you really love, something in which you have invested so much of yourself, that you feel yourself to be a master of that craft. Consider the relationship between a carpenter and wood. The master carpenter knows the difference between teak and oak, pine and maple, knows which way to carve with the grain and how to move the plane by the feel and smell of the plank.

Imagine yourself as the carpenter. All your senses are alive to the wood! Your nostrils recognize the tang of sawdust and resin. You know the firm heartwood by feel, the hew of rough timbers and the silken strokes of hand-rubbed oils that massage smooth surfaces to silky sheen. This is a deep dimension of mastery. This relationship is more like that of lover and beloved than of lord and vassal! The wood sculptor who takes the chisel to the block must so love the wood that it becomes an extension of his or her own being. The wood responds to the hands of the sculptor as if to a caress, and becomes art.

Consider a master potter, who takes an inert lump of clay and, working it on the wheel, feels the clay leap and rise into her hands. Neither the clay nor the potter is complete without the other. Each finds fulfillment in the dance that calls them both into being.

In the Jewish High Holy Day liturgy, in the prayer texts *Ki Hineh k'Chomer* and *Ki Anu Amekha*, this quality of mutual divine-human aliveness appears as a central theme. When we are like clay, Yours are the Potter's hands; when we become fine silver, we are refined in Your Presence. At times we are like the molten glass receiving the Blower's breath. When the face we turn to You is "need for guidance," You turn toward us the quality of the Shepherd; when we need comfort, You become the Consoler; when we need strength, You become the Empowerer. Each time our own needs turn, the appropriate facet of You turns to face us. As the clay rises to the potter's hands, we rise in Your hands.

One especially fruitful way to work with the experience of *Adon* is to extract the term from the realm of master-over, out of our master/slave consciousness into the realm of our relationship with God in the great artistic project of creation. One of the most moving cinematic vignettes I ever saw depict this theme was in the film *From Mao to Mozart,* a documentary account of a visit to China by the great violinist Isaac Stern at the end of the Cultural Revolution. In a poignant moment of the film, Stern is listening to a young girl execute a technically flawless rendition of a Mozart piece. When she finishes, he gently takes her violin and plays the piece again. The room is hushed as the violin comes alive in his hands. His notes are identical to hers, but suddenly they have become magical, resonant with the deepest feeling. The melodies leap, soar, sing, cry. When Stern finishes, the astonished audience is in awe. Then, turning to the young girl, he says, "You see, you don't play the violin; it plays you. No, more than that. You and the violin become one instrument and something else plays both of you."

This scene offered me a transformative insight into the nature of the relationship we call *Adon.* I imagine myself the violin. What if the violin were aware? What would I experience as a violin in Isaac Stern's hands, feeling those fingers and that heart open to me so that we become one in a cascade of music? Through that embrace I open and become one, not only with the *Adon* but with the Power that plays us both.

The relationship to our *Adon* is one of intimate receptivity. To experience God in the aspect of *Adon* is to heighten our receptivity to what God is calling us to do and become. When the name *Adonay* is understood to derive from this sense of *Adon,* it is not entirely surprising that Jewish tradition associates *Adonay* with the *Shekhinah,* the feminine aspect of God! Throughout Jewish mystical and hasidic literature, *Adonay* is described as the portal through which the Divine Flow enters the world. Reciprocally, it is also the portal through which the seeker of the divine realm must pass. *Adonay* names the gate, the "Place," where the spiritual and physical realms touch, the semiporous membrane filtering the ceaseless divine flow of *shefa* from the higher realms directly into the realm of physicality.

This feminine aspect of God receives the many streams from above, unifying, perfecting, and transforming them so that divinity can irrigate the world. We have learned to know her by many names. She is *Shekhinah,* the power dwelling within and among us; She is *Malkhut,* Kingdom; She is the Well, the Gate, the Moon, the Sacred City of Jerusalem, King David, Rachel and Leah, the Bride, Shabbat, and *Adonay.*

Yosef Gikatilla writes: "From the Name יהוה all the channels flow and are drawn to *Adonay . . .* the great sustainer of all Creation. All who wish to experience union with the Name יהוה Ever Blessed, go forth and enter through the mouth [of this gate]. *Adonay* is the way."

The Chernobyler Rebbe adds: "The [God within the] human self is called by the name *Adonay,* also called *Shekhinah,* for she dwells within the lower realms. . . . The Presence of the Creator fills the earth. No place is empty! Yet the Presence takes the form of garments: God is clothed by all physical things. This aspect of Divinity is called *Shekhinah,* the Presence-that-dwells-within, since it dwells within everything—and is called *Adonay."* She is the gate of which the *Zohar* speaks: "One who enters must enter through this gate."

The Chernobyler Rebbe was investigating the mystical teachings about the name *Adonay.* One day as he was reading Torah he encountered an obscure word in the detailed description of the building of the *Mishkan,* the exquisitely crafted Tabernacle holding the tablets of the Ten Commandments. The word was *adanim,* usually translated as "ball-joints" or "sockets." A ball-joint, the Rebbe mused, is a mechanism for flexible connection. Just as the flexible *adanim* held the upper and lower sections of the *Mishkan* together, so too *Adonay* holds the lower and higher worlds together. "Since the whole world is garbed in God," he said, "and God is within each garment, this must refer to the aspect of divinity we call *Adonay*. Like the *adanim* which held the *Mishkan* together, *Adonay* is divinity as it filters down into the physical realm so that we can reunite it with its Source. In every act of worship, whether study, prayer, eating, or drinking, we can bring about this reunification!"

—◦⟨⟩◦—

Jewish tradition offers us the opportunity to take this exploration still further. In Hebrew the word *adan* also means "threshold," a point of entry. Although "threshold" suggests a bridging partition at an entrance, we also speak of a threshold when we refer to the outer limit of capacity: we cannot go beyond the threshold.

When we call out to God as *Adonay*, we can imagine our soul ushered to the threshold of our capacity for intimacy with the Divine Presence; to the limit of our capacity to be open to God's love, light, and power. In order to take the next step, we must risk stretching ourselves past our prior limits, expanding our willingness to receive God's embrace and be received into God. Each time we do our most rigorous spiritual stretching; each time we go to the most vulnerable places in our souls and allow love into hurt and unhealed places; each time we reveal aspects of self not yet uncovered, we are loved by God as *Adonay*, our Threshold.

Yotzeyr, Borey, Ha'Rachaman, M'kor Ha'Chayyim, Shekhinah, Yah, Adonay . . . we sing with the author of *Shir Ha'Kavod*, the mystical "Hymn of Glory": "Through countless visions, the images come. Behold, through all the visions, You are One!"

יהוה

אלהנו

It is therefore written:"Hide, I will hide My face."
That is, God will be hidden
so that they do not even know God is there.
But once a person knows God is hidden,
God is not really hidden.

—BAAL SHEM TOV

I am closer to you than yourself,
Than your soul, than your own breath.
Why do you not see me?
Why do you not hear me?

—IBN AL ARABI

ברוך אתה יהוה **אלהנו** מלך העולם

A Fountain of Blessings are You
The-Eternal-Breath-of-Life-Beyond-and-Within,
Divine Expansiveness Concentrated within our World.

Eloheynu

❧〰❧

With so few words we have thus far awakened so much within ourselves! We have each turned on our own fountain of blessings and learned to stand in receptivity and wonder beneath its flow. We have opened our hands to receive and give. We have begun to find the divine sparks within all creation. We have learned to call out to God and to face God as a power not only beyond but also within us. With humility and vulnerability we stand within the mystery. With each breath we say the Name-that-transcends-name and link ourselves anew to the eternal rhythm of life. We call out: You, the Eternal-Breath-of-All-Life, the Wholly One, You are our Power. *Adonay*, you are *Eloheynu*. *Our* God. Our *Elohim*.

In the wilderness, the people of Israel hear God's instruction through Moshe: "I am יהוה your *Elohim* who calls you out of

Mitzrayim, the narrow places of your lives, to be your *Elohim.* I am
יהוה your *Elohim."* It is not the first time we have heard these words.
Engraved on the tablets of stone Moshe brought down the moun-
tain was a first "commandment," *"Anokhi* יהוה *Elohekha:* I am יהוה
your *Elohim."* What does it mean that יהוה is called *Elohim?* Does it
surprise you that translating *Elohim* as "God" is not sufficient?

Shema Yisrael יהוה *Eloheynu,* יהוה *Echad!*
Fully comprehend, You-who-wrestle-with-God,
יהוה is *Eloheynu,* (our *Elohim*),
יהוה is a Complete Unity!

Anokhi יהוה *Elohekha*
I am יהוה *Elohekha,* your *Elohim.*

Barukh Ata יהוה *Eloheynu . . .*
A Fountain of Blessings are You whose Name is The-Eternal-
Breath-of-Life-Beyond-and-Within, *Eloheynu,* our *Elohim . . .*

What is *Elohim?* We know that each Name of God, each facet of
the crystal, introduces us to another quality of God. Through the
Name יהוה we glimpse the infinite, even as the ineffable force
infusing the universe with vitality and consciousness remains
entirely beyond our grasp. Through the Name *Adonay* we are invited
to approach the *Shekhinah* and the threshold of a most intimate
experience of the Divine Presence. Now our *brakha,* and other
sources as well, insist that יהוה must also be comprehended as
Elohim, indeed as our *Elohim—Eloheynu.* What is the meaning of this
Name? What quality of God is *Elohim?*

—◦◦◦—

In his famous work *Sha'ar Ha'Yichud V'Ha'Emunah*, "The Gate of Unity and Faith," Rabbi Schneur Zalman of Liadi, the founder of *CHaBaD* Hasidism, made accessible a new synthesis of Jewish spiritual and kabbalistic teaching. Rabbi Schneur Zalman approached the same question we are asking, not directly, but through what might seem like a side door.

Perhaps impelled by the injunction that we understand *Elohim* in relationship to the Name as יהוה, the great rabbi also begins with the meaning of the unpronounceable Name. יהוה, he reminds us, is "That-which-calls-everything-into-being," the life-force flowing through all creatures and calling forth their existence out of nothingness. The rabbi opens with a quotation from Deuteronomy praising יהוה as *Ha'Gadol* and *Ha'Gibor*, "Great and Mighty." These words, he sets out to show, are not merely words of praise, but kabbalistic descriptions of processes within divinity through which we can come to know the quality of God revealed as *Elohim*.

"Great," he reminds us, refers to the expansive divine attribute of unlimited, unrestricted giving, called *chesed*. *Chesed* is God suffusing all the worlds with life without restraint. *Chesed* is the boundless outpouring of divine desire to give. "Might," on the other hand, refers to the energy of constriction or withdrawal, also called *tzimtzum*, which contains and circumscribes the rush of life-force.

Through *tzimtzum* the full and unbearable intensity of God's unrestrained energy is reduced, cooled, and modulated. Through *tzimtzum* the divine light is so condensed within the world and within living creatures that matter appears to exist apart from the spiritual energy within it. The divine attribute of *gevurah* condenses the *chesed*-flow of light and life-force, concealing it within materiality, so that creatures can live and matter exist screened from the intensity of the very forces providing the source of their existence. Through the quality of "might" divine light is shielded, hidden, so that our lives are possible.

Deep within us is a concealed yet manifest power, which glows just enough that its light can be revealed when we still our minds and open our hearts. We are invited to be holy explorers, seeking and discovering God *mit'tzamtzeym b'kol davar*, God's presence hidden everywhere, just below the surface.

Kabbalah describes the universe as an exquisite paradox. On the one hand, God has withdrawn from the bubble of the universe in order to make room for creation. This "pullback" of God's infinite Self is the *tzimtzum* permitting the outwardly separate existence of the universe. However, God's light is also condensed within the world, concentrated within every speck of matter and wave of energy. "There is no place empty of God," says the *Tikkuney Zohar.* God's nearness may be less than obvious, but this is all part of the game. As the medieval master Kabbalist Moshe Cordovero proclaimed: "The essence of divinity is found in every single thing, for nothing but God exists!" And so, says the Baal Shem Tov, "When a person realizes that God is hidden, God is really not so hidden at all! The [perceptual] barriers crumble . . . and then nothing can separate that person from God."

God, to our astonishment, is at once both radically distant and radically present, both context and content, surrounding and filling: *sovev* and *memaley.* God is both hands of the *aleph*, hiding from the universe in order to create it and hiding within the universe in order to sustain it.

The name *Elohim* represents this quality of *tzimtzum*, the One Source modulating the intensity of the pure blazing light, organizing and restricting life-force and consciousness so that its full intensity is shielded and life is protected. *Elohim* is the ultimate power of the cosmos (א *aleph*) guided and channeled (ל *lamed*) into life (ה *hey*) and toward (י *yod*) abundant generativity (ם *mem*). (More on the letters *lamed* and *mem* follows in the chapter on *Melekh*.)

Thus, says Rabbi Schneur Zalman, Psalm 84 teaches us that "יהוה *Elohim* is a sun and a shield." As יהוה, God is compared to the sun, a pure blaze of Being. As *Elohim*, God is a protective shield, preserving life. I sometimes like to translate this phrase "יהוה *Elohim* is the sun and the sunscreen." The sun provides the fiery light and heat that give us life and health, and sunscreen limits the intensity of exposure so that the sun's rays are beneficial and safe. I need the sun and I need the shield. As the lenses of some sunglasses adjust to the level of brightness, darkening and lightening in proportion to the intensity of ambient light, divinity too is a self-regulating power. This is the quality we call *Elohim*.

When we are in touch with the *Elohim* aspect of the divine, we discover that divine self-restraint, withdrawal, and constriction, far from being negative, are as full an expression of God's love as is God's *chesed*. Both are essential for our flourishing.

As creatures in the divine image, we can also recognize *chesed* and *gevurah* within ourselves. We too are givers and withholders. It may be easy to imagine that only generous and unrestrained giving is love, and that we should never hold back or constrict ourselves. Perhaps we believe that to be fully present to another person we need to be fully "on" all the time. The lesson of *Elohim* is that love manifests in the restraint of *gevurah* as much as within the stream of *chesed*.

We can cultivate *tzimtzum* in our relationships, sensitively modulating our intensity so that the "thou" we encounter can know and feel our love and still have enough room to thrive. How destructive we can be when we subject others to the full force of our feelings without regard for what they can handle. This may be more clearly true with anger or pain, but it is true as well when the feeling is love. Giving means respecting the integrity of the receiver. We must remember that whatever we give, we are offering it to one whose being also needs room to breathe emotionally.

Perhaps you have already learned this lesson from feeling invaded or smothered by another's intensity. Someone's desire to give or guide may have begun with the best of intentions, but increasingly you felt there was less and less room for you. The giver was not really aware of your limits and behaved as if you were merely an extension of his or her own desire. Or perhaps you yourself have been the uncontrolled "giver" whose friend, child, or lover was overwhelmed, and withdrew or incomprehensibly fled from you.

For parents, this can be an especially hard lesson. It is so easy to fall into the trap of treating a child as an extension of one's own self. After all, in utero that was literally true. It can be difficult to separate and allow a new individual to develop his or her own identity. A lesson of *Elohim* is that in lovingly "holding back" we can plant our love deep in the hearts of those we care for.

From *Elohim* we learn that love includes good boundaries. We and all Creation may be One in God, but in the created world each being's life depends on God's Self-restraint. To truly love you, I must learn to discern where my "I" ends and your "you" begins. In a mature personality, boundless giving and disciplined self-restraint find a harmonious balance.

At the close of every Jewish service, these lines of the prayer *Aleynu* express this awareness. "Comprehend this today," we sing, "and meditate upon this in your heart: יהוה is *Elohim:* The boundless giving power that calls everything into being is radically present, condensed, and hidden in all existence, in the heavens above and on the earth below," loving us through self-restraint. As physical beings, we may not be able to grasp the full intensity of divine power, but we each know we hold a shimmering spark of that power within us. יהוה is *Elohim.* The revealed and the concealed are One.

מלך

Through "kingship," God comes in contact with the people.
It is written: "From my flesh I see God."
From the physical we can perceive the spiritual.
Such physical pleasure results from human union!
Thus we can understand the delight a person can have
in union with God.

—BAAL SHEM TOV

Oh wonder of wonders!
When I think of the union of the soul with God! . . .
The divine love=spring surges over the soul,
sweeping her out of herself into the unnamed being
of her original source. . . .
In this exalted state she has lost her proper self
and is flowing full=flood
into the unity of the divine nature. . . .
There she is no more called soul:
she is called infinite being.

—MEISTER ECKHART

ברוך אתה יהוה אלהנו **מלך** העולם

A Fountain of Blessings are You
The-Eternal-Breath-of-Life-Beyond-and-Within,
Concentrated Divine Expansiveness within our World,
Channeling Creative Power to Manifest

Melekh

♥⚬⌒⚬♥

Melekh, usually translated "King," is a central image in Jewish liturgy and theology. Generations of Jewish spiritual storytellers wove their lessons about the relationship of the people Israel and God into parables of countless variation, telling of the patient King whose wayward children must struggle with separation, loss, and longing before they find their way home. In the liturgy of the High Holy Days, the image of God as King assumes awesome proportions as the liturgy builds toward the fullest acknowledgment of the *Malkhut*, the sovereignty, of God.

Yet *melekh* is a challenging word. Kingship is not a notion that sits well with the American ideal of a democratic community of equal citizens. The United States came into being in opposition to monarchy and by virtue of its defeat. The power we wish to serve is not a despotic king. Nor do we view ourselves as subjects. We may easily feel insulted by this imagery.

We are often further injured and discomfited by the gendered quality of the translation. There is no reigning "queen of heaven," only a "king." The male ruler-God words of traditional religious liturgy neither reflect nor evoke the God we seek. In my work as a rabbi and teacher, I am often confronted with the dissonance that words like *Adonay* as Lord and *Melekh* as King evoke in spiritual seekers. This dissonance has prompted a creative calling forth of other images from traditional sources and personal inspiration. And yet, it is precisely our discomfort with images of *Melekh* "King" and *Malkhut* "Kingdom," images so woven into the fabric of Jewish prayer-language and theology, that calls us to wrestle more deeply with this troublesome word.

Beyond Big Daddy

If we are to free ourselves from the most limiting uses of *Melekh*, we must revisit our own childhoods. For many of us, our initial exposure to this word came through the God-language that was taught to us as children. When we were young, Bible stories and prayers offered us an image of God mirroring the relationship of parent and child. Perhaps you too can close your eyes and recall those pictures planted in your earliest memories. The "King" has a long white beard, is sometimes warm and loving, frequently stern and powerful, perhaps even frightening.

A vignette: One morning during the festival of *Sukkot* my husband took a class from a local synagogue into the leafy *sukkah*, asking the kids, "Where is God?" They all pointed toward the sky. "God is in the sky?" he challenged them. "Is there any possibility that God is here with us in the *sukkah*? Any possibility that the fingers pointing to the sky could also point to us?" The children were bewildered. No teacher had spoken like this before. It is a tragedy that the image of a Disneyland king on a lofty throne is reinforced to such a degree that it occludes all other possible experiences.

We grow older, but too often it is our eight-year-old God that remains with us, and we wonder why our theology doesn't serve us very well. For many, religious instruction ends at thirteen. The opportunity to do any more sophisticated spiritual work is rarely available, and we assume that the eight-to-thirteen-year-old version is all religious tradition offers. We are stuck with God on the level of Santa Claus and Casper the friendly ghost.

We may abandon God entirely when those images become inadequate for the adults we have become. It is hardly surprising then when we return to religious tradition with a mature consciousness, the Old Man on the throne is the first object of our egalitarian/feminist impulses. We very legitimately join Rabbi Shefa Gold as she sings, "No more Big Daddy; the monarchy is dead. . . ." The skybound King forced upon us as children rules no more.

To reclaim a spiritually deep Jewish identity, we must do some house-cleaning of these dust-ridden images left over from our childhood. However, I want first to acknowledge that there is a legitimate place for some of them. As much as we need to reject the oppressive legacy of the Royal Man in the Sky, our soul does have a need for a powerful, loving, and protecting papa—even perhaps for an angry, limit-setting papa, although here we have to be exceptionally careful, for this image can easily overwhelm and become abusive.

The Papa/King image, if taught and lived well by loving, patient, strong, gentle fathers, can be an anchor, offering an important gift to a part of the soul. The child we were remains within us; it does not disappear as we mature. When we understand that our inner child is alive within us, we need not discard its imagery. We never finish needing a caring father, an *Av Ha'Rachamim*, who, with love, holds firm boundaries, punishes wrong, and defends us. These are qualities we ultimately internalize in order to feel secure and internally worthy. Structureless, permissive parenting in the name of love does not help any child acquire internal balance and confidence.

However, angry, punitive fathering, stressing submission to callous authority, is destructive. Those of us who were offered only a frightening and punishing male God/parent must heal from childhood "God-abuse" by parents and teachers who used "God" to reflect their own experiences of victimization and rage.

Yet even a wise-loving-strong-powerful Papa/King God is insufficient. So part of the work of reclaiming our capacity to be in relationship with God is acquiring a theological vocabulary matching our emotional and intellectual maturity, and responsive to our adult needs. Here the word *Melekh* becomes centrally important precisely because it is one of the most frozen and problematic images we have; for the double-barreled shotgun of feminist and egalitarian critiques, it makes an easy target. We will not reclaim a mature *Melekh* by an "end run" around its simplistic imagery. We must proceed with a willingness to engage it directly and deeply.

Power That Serves

We can begin by working with the letters, as we did with *barukh.*
Melekh is spelled מלך: מ *mem,* ל *lamed,* and כ *khaf* (which at the
end of the word appears in its final form ך). Let us begin by
working backward. *Melekh* ends with the letter, כ *khaf,* which we
encountered in *barukh.* There we saw that *khaf* was a "vessel" letter, meaning "hands open to receive and give." Recall that in the
word *barukh, khaf* was preceded by two other letters from the same
triad. Each of the three letters in *barukh* is about filling, holding,
and pouring out; all point to teachings about being or becoming
such a vessel.

There is also an unusual pattern in the letters of *melekh.* In the
following chart, you can see that the letters מ *mem,* ל *lamed,* and כ
khaf are in sequence.

When we approach the letters of the Hebrew alphabet as
dynamically evolving divine energies, we see that the letters *khaf,*
lamed, and *mem* flow like a stream. The *khaf,* the "hands-that-open-
to-receive-and-then-pour-into-the-next-outstretched" is preceded
by *mem* and *lamed.* The word is a ribbon unfurling toward us, inviting us to follow it back to the Source. What can the letters teach
us about the Source?

מ *Mem,* the opening letter of *Melekh,* when spelled out fully
consists of two *mems* מם. *MeM* is the letter of water, in Hebrew
מים *MayiM, Mem-Yod-Mem.* (Both מם *mem* and מים *mayim* typically
employ the concluding *mem* in final form: ם) *MayiM,* water, also
suggests *yaM* ocean, *ayM* mother and *iMa* "mama." *Mem* invites us
to dive into the "mother waters." *Mem, mayim, yam, aym.* Perhaps we

ALEPH	BEYT/ VEYT	GIMMEL	DALET	HEY	WAW	ZAYIN	CHET	TET
א	ב	ג	ד	ה	ו	ז	ח	ט
silent letter	Has sound of B or V	Has sound of G	Has sound of D	Has sound of H	Has sound of W (V in modern Hebrew)	Has sound of Z	Has sound of gutteral CH	Has sound of T
1	2	3	4	5	6	7	8	9

YOD	KAF/ KHAF	LAMED	MEM	NUN	SAMEKH	AYIN	PEY/ FEY	TZADI
י	כ	ל	מ	נ	ס	ע	פ	צ
Has sound of Y	Has sound of K or guttural KH	Has sound of L	Has sound of M	Has sound of N	Has sound of S	silent letter	Has sound of P or F	Has sound of TZ
10	20	30	40	50	60	70	80	90

KOF	REYSH	SIN/ SHIN	TAV	FINAL KHAF	FINAL MEM	FINAL NUN	FINAL FAY	FINAL TZADI
ק	ר	ש	ת	ך	ם	ן	ף	ץ
Has sound of K	Has sound of R	Has sound of S or SH	Has sound of T	Has sound of KH at the end of a word	Has sound of M at the end of a word	Has sound of N at the end of a word	Has sound of F at the end of a word	Has sound of TZ at the end of a word
100	200	300	400					

could call *mem* the letter of the maternal waters of creation. Mother-waters are waters of birthing, womb waters, if you will. The letter *mem* points us toward a uniquely maternal aspect of God, giving us a glimpse of the Source as the "womb of Creation."

The letter *mem* evokes the primordial seas from which all life emerges. *Mem*-waters teem with life, with creativity and generativity. On earth we know these waters as the fertile seas nurturing microscopic life over eons toward complexity and diversity. These are the waters that birth all life. The Hebrew letter *mem* evokes all that is fluid, creative, and fertile, including "the heavens," in Hebrew שמים *shamayim*, "the realm which is *sheh-mayim* fluid." The lower waters and the upper waters are, in this way, one realm. From these God-waters life issues forth.

What else can we say about water? Coming from a tap, it is a small stream, but it is also the source of fecundity and prolific birthing, a place of tremendous strength. No matter how great the turbulence at the surface of the sea, below there is utter calm. Recalling that each letter is a quality of God, as a creature in the divine image I seek those qualities within my self. No matter how great a tempest rages about me, there is a place in my soul where I can find the calm of deep *mayim*, where the water is still and powerful.

ל *Lamed* is the letter of teaching and guidance. *LaMaD* is the root of the verb meaning both "to teach" and "to learn." A *melamed* is a teacher; a *talmid* is a student; the Talmud is a repository of learning; a *lamdan* is a great scholar. "*Lamed*" is to instruct on the way to go, to guide, or to be guided. I have always thought it quite wonderful that *lamed* is such a crooked letter. It is like a path. I remember looking at it and saying to myself, "Is there even a single life whose path is straight?" Our lives have so many curves and turns. We hold faith that as our life paths wind we will secure the help we need. *Lamed* is the letter of guidance along the not-straight path.

When we bring *mem* and *lamed* together with *khaf* we can read *Melekh* in this way: the maternal waters, source of creativity from which all life issues forth *(mem)*, are channeled and guided *(lamed)*, toward the hand/vessel that is open to receive and give *(khaf)*. *Melekh* takes us from source through channel to ourselves as receivers and givers.

Now that I work so much with a computer, I have begun to enjoy framing the divine attribute of *Melekh* in the role of server, linking the realms of beyond and within, not unlike the "server" connecting me, the humble computer user, to the Internet. When I "surf the Web," I link-in through a server company that both I and the Web need to make that link possible. *Melekh* is that aspect of God providing the link for us to go "on line."

When we open our hearts with desire for God, we set in motion the flow of God toward us. The flow is guided toward us and back through *Melekh*. When we hope for guidance, for learning, for wisdom, we yearn toward that aspect of God we know as *Melekh*. *Melekh* is that place within us where the Self of God and our own selves touch.

Reb Zalman, when teaching about *Melekh*, would often remind us that Hebrew employs two very different words for "ruler." *Melekh* is one, but the other is *sar*. A *sar* is an autocrat. A *melekh* has a counselor. A *sar* rules without consultation; a human *melekh* is like a constitutional monarch. As *melekh*, King David could be instructed, even chastised and punished, by the prophet Nathan. Torah requires a *melekh* to be instructed in Torah every night, particularly stressing those passages limiting the *melekh*'s powers and recalling that a *melekh* is always subject to, and must act in accordance with, God's law.

An earthly *melekh* is a conduit, a server. This is perhaps why in some ancient cultures a king was mythologized as a semidivine, semihuman figure. To have access to someone part-god/part-human is to have access to a point on the physical plane where the world of spirit and the world of matter touch. The king who has entry into both realms becomes the window, the channel, the "interface." Through the person of the demigod king, the divine and the human commingle.

Our people never regarded a human *melekh* as anything other than human. Yet we retained an understanding of *melekh* as an "interface." The *melekh* holds the connection open; the *melekh* is the conduit; the *melekh* serves. Thus, it is not surprising that we called the portal through which divinity flows into physicality *Malkhut* "kingdom."

Like *Adonay*, *Malkhut* (and even King David!) also became associated with *Shekhinah*, the feminine presence of God, the sluice-gate of divine energy's flow into materiality, where the upper waters rush into the sea of our souls and our world. In the notion of *Melekh* and *Malkhut*, shades of maleness and femaleness again combine. The maternal waters from above flow through the masculine channel to the feminine *Malkhut* and into the world. The feminine is the river and the well. *Malkhut* is *Shekhinah*, the threshold, the "Place" of the semipermeable membrane between divine and human realms.

The Jewish High Holy Day drama ritually enthrones *Melekh* and proclaims divine *Malkhut*. With liturgical song and chant, we invoke and draw the *Melekh* toward us to "sit" on the "throne." We use this imagery to become especially receptive to power elevating us to conscious connection. In Kabbalah, "sitting" is a code word for the descending flow of God-energy into the world: the movement of God from utterly beyond to utterly within. When we call out to the *Melekh* to "sit upon the throne," we call out our souls' longing to receive and be in that flow. We strive to be truly receptive, to become so empty of self-conscious ego that we can be full of God. Then we become the "throne."

The Jewish mystical tradition teaches that divinity flows into the world through desire, ours as well as God's. That desire is mutual and reciprocal, like the desire of lovers for each other. Creation itself, we have learned, is a product of this desire. God's longing to be seen, to be known and recognized; God's hope to call out and be called back to, is met by our reciprocal desire. As the Talmud observes, "Even more than the calf wants to nurse, the cow wants to give suck."

And so as our prayers "rise," the upward movement of our longing creates what Reb Zalman describes as "a cosmic updraft," stimulating "a cosmic downdraft" and opening the *Melekh* channel. Then *Melekh* descends by way of *Shekhinah*, the Divine Presence, into the world.

I once had the opportunity to visit a house designed by the brilliant solar architect Carlos Romero-Fredes. It was not a house with solar collectors; the structure itself was a solar collector without any auxiliary heating system. Under the ground, where the temperature is a constant 50 degrees, a long conduit snaked down through the soil from a grating on the slab floor of the house above, until it surfaced in a distant field. As the temperature inside the house rose from the sunlight penetrating the massive skylights, a hot updraft surged through the ceiling vents. The updraft evacuated the hot air and the resulting vacuum sucked cool 50-degree air from the conduit into the house. Thus the house both self-cooled and self-heated. It required no fossil fuels, no back-up system of any kind. The house simply "breathed."

Just as natural convection breathed the air through this house, with prayer we breathe divinity through us. We warm ourselves with our prayer, our inner fire is fanned, and as our prayers and longing for God rise, our souls expand. The divine energy is drawn into us, into our *khaf*, our dwelling, our soul-vessel.

Kabbalah teaches that we can become the "throne." Becoming a throne is both a personal and a communal spiritual endeavor. We must be willing to let go of our attachment to negative habits of mind and body, to purify our desires and clarify our intentions. So many of us live with minds and hearts clogged with resentments, old angers and fears. We cling to old habits of thinking and being until those habits begin to define who we are. Yet we fear that without them we would lose our selves.

The irony is, of course, that only when we let go of what is old is there room to receive the new. We are born to be whole, to be free, to be loved and filled by the presence of God. When we give up the obsessive clutter, we make room to be filled by God. Then we rise out of our petty *mochin d'katnut*, our small-mindedness, and receive in fullness the *mochin d'gadlut*, expanded mind.

With heart, soul, and mind open and receptive, we surrender control and ask only to be filled with God. We let go of expectations and find profound insight. We release our judgments and are filled with radiant divine light. We relinquish our attachment to external goals and discover true purpose. We exchange self-satisfied cleverness for the beginnings of wisdom.

Melekh: movement of divine creative power through its pathway to fill the receptive soul.

העולם

The Name יהוה is beyond all Time.
Was‑ness—is‑ness—will‑be‑ness
All in one transcendental moment!
So too, above whatever we can know of Space.
For the One at every moment
calls forth Space itself
out of Nothingness:
The Above, the Below, and all directions.
The One is above Time and Space,
yet exists within them too
In constant union with *Malkhut,*
From which Time and Space arise.

—RABBI SCHNEUR ZALMAN OF LIADI

A blinding spark flashed
within the concealed of the concealed
From the mystery of the infinite
a cluster of vapor in formlessness. . . .
Under the impact of breaking through,
one high and hidden point shone.
Beyond that point nothing is known.
So it is called "Beginning."

—*ZOHAR*

ברוך אתה יהוה אלהנו מלך העולם

A Fountain of Blessings are You
The-Eternal-Breath-of-Life-Beyond-and-Within,
Divine Expansiveness Concentrated within our World,
Channeling Creative Power to Manifest
as the Mystery of Consciousness becoming Time-Space.

Ha'Olam

❦

Ha'Olam brings us back to the beginning of our *brakha*, where God's creative desire flashes forth from the infinite Oneness of *aleph* to form a *beyt*. Within this expanding *beyt* the nascent universe unfolds, born of God's desire to be known and offer love. *Olam* brings us back to our beginning. The Infinite One speaks Creation into existence, at once withdrawing from Creation and penetrating deep within it. As time and space unfurl, cascades of frenzied elementary particles emerge and perish, combine and recombine, collapse and explode. Vast galactic clouds coalesce; stars burning for billions of years implode in cosmic cataclysms. Supernovas hurl their stellar matter far into space. New fireball stars form to burn for billions of years. Some stars host planets, some perhaps will support matter in its evolutionary urge toward life. Upon at least one planet, life awakens to consciousness and turns to face God, *Melekh* of the *Olam*—Power of the universe.

⁓◦◉◦⁓

Olam is a curious word. Like the "universe" it describes, it is multidimensional. To *lamed* and *mem* it adds an ע *ayin*, the letter that means "eye": divine vision, imagination, and vast creativity. *Ayin* is the eye of God that envisions and embraces all possibilities. In the divine eye, a universe of potentialities awaits the chance to flash into life.

Olam is frequently translated "world" or "universe" as in *Ha'Olam*, pointing toward the realm of space: <u>The</u> *Olam*, the universe and all its worlds or, closer to home, the "universe" of our planet Earth. *L'Olam*, however, is always translated "forever." *L'Olam*, <u>toward</u> *Olam*, expresses the dimension, not of space but of time. What is *Olam* that we can use it to refer to either time or space? Is it space or time . . . or is it both?

This query may seem familiar. During this century Albert Einstein, the Jewish mathematician and physicist, turned the Western world's thinking about time and space upside down with his demonstration that they are not separate, as classical physics had presumed, but a continuum. Neither time nor space exists separate from the other. Space and time "inter-are."

How delicious that for millennia prior to Einstein's mathematical proofs Jewish tradition has used the word *Olam*, "space-time," to express this very insight. What a pleasure to find in *Olam* a single word encompassing this mind-expanding "aha!" It may seem outrageous, but you can see how the Hebrew could give us permission to experiment in translating *Melekh Ha'Olam* so much more expansively than "King of the Universe." We could say "Serving

Power, Conduit of *Ayn Sof* (the Infinite), into Time-Space." But that is not all.

Beyond Time and Space

With the appearance of the light,
the universe expanded.
With concealment of the light,
all things that exist were created in their variety.
This is the mystery of the act of creation.
One who understands will understand.

—SHIMON LAVI

The word *Olam* invites us to visit the time-space continuum and extend the limits of what we can learn about the universe. The meaning of *Olam* carries a challenge for us. While *Olam* expresses the unity of time and space, a further layer of meaning lies secreted behind even this concept. The root letters of *Olam* mean "hidden" or "concealed" (see p. 97). Something *ne'elam* is closed, secret, or disappeared from view, as though behind a locked door. "With concealment . . . all is created." We live within a mystery we cannot penetrate. Concealed are the farthest reaches of time and space, past and future, the endlessly vast and the endlessly small. Einstein said:

> In our endeavor to understand reality we are somewhat like a man trying to understand the mechanism of a closed watch. He sees the face and the moving hands, even hears its ticking, but he has no way of opening the case. If he is ingenious he may form some picture of a mechanism which could be responsible for all the things he

observes, but he may never be quite sure his picture is the only one which could explain his observations.

The universe is *ne'elam*, a locked door, a hidden mystery, and yet it invites our participation. We gaze with wonder at the night sky, barely grasping that the stars we see are a tiny fraction of those just within our galaxy. Astronomers estimate there are over a hundred billion stars in our galaxy alone. With the aid of high-powered telescopes we can discern distant pinpoints of light that are not stars but entire galaxies themselves. We are in the orbit of a star on the periphery of one of those galaxies. The universe as a whole, we are told, may contain a hundred billion galaxies.

An illustration offered by Peter Russell, in his work *Global Brain*, helps us apprehend the unfathomable scale of the universe. "If we imagine the North American continent to represent our galaxy," he says, "then the Earth would be a mere ten-thousandth of an inch, and its orbit the size of a pinhead; the sun would be the minutest speck visible to the naked eye in the center of this pinhead; the volume occupied by the whole solar system would be about the size of an apple, hidden somewhere in North America. . . . Yet this galaxy is but itself a minute structure in the whole universe, another apple lost on a huge continent." The universe is *ne'elam*, a hidden mystery.

We do not even know what the universe is made of. Although we can find in distant stars all the physical elements we know of from our own world, biologist Rupert Sheldrake points out that "One of the most surprising and puzzling features of the universe revealed by modern cosmology is that most of the matter in it is utterly unknown to us—'dark matter.' . . . This dark matter has powerful gravitational effects, but its constitution is unknown. Recent estimates of the amount of dark matter in the universe vary from around 90 to 99 percent.... The magnitude of this mystery is staggering. The great majority of the matter in the universe is utterly unknown." The *Olam* is *ne'elam*, a hidden mystery.

And yet, though our earth is less than a minute speck in a pinhead solar system within vast billions of galaxies, it is itself a universe, its untold billions of pinhead atoms made of further countless billions of micro-speck subatomic particles. The realms of inner space are as vast as the outer, as Gary Zukav illustrates in his masterful work *The Dancing Wu Li Masters:* "The smallest object that we can see, even under a microscope, contains millions of atoms. To see atoms in a baseball, we would have to make the baseball the size of the earth. [Then] its atoms would be about the size of grapes.... The nucleus of an atom as high as a fourteen-story building would be about the size of a grain of salt.... This gives us the scale of sub-atomic particles."

The universe is *ne'elam*, the ultimate magical mystery tour. Yet this mind-spin is still not the full extent of the secret. So far we can still imagine we are touring actual material "realities," however incomprehensibly vast or small. Yet in the mystery of the universe, even "reality" itself is not at all as it appears.

The Quantum Revolution Turns Everything We Think We Know About "Reality" Inside Out

We all grew up with Newtonian physics, the branch of science that offered rational and comprehensive explanations for the behavior of the phenomena of the natural world. In the Newtonian universe, everything from planets to baseballs was subject to the same universal principles. The revolution caused by quantum physics lies in the discovery that these trusted "laws of Nature," which explain phenomena around us so well, do not apply in the realm of the ultra-small.

On the subatomic level, even the existence of particles is being questioned. Indeed, when we approach the most fundamental constituent parts of existence, it appears that nothing actually exists at all apart from our interaction with it. When we measure or observe an electron, for example, it appears like a "thing" existing in a "place," but when we are not looking it loses its materiality. It becomes an energy which can spread to more than one place, disappear entirely, and then reappear elsewhere as a particle as soon as we look again. Electrons can disappear from one energy orbit around a nucleus and appear instantly somewhere else, *without traveling* in between. They apparently blip out of "space-time" entirely. They go "nowhere" in "no-time."

This phenomenon causes physicists to question: Is there even a "there" when we are not looking? Many are beginning to say that there is not. They believe that in between appearances, in between what physicists call "quantum jumps," an electron leaps not through time-space but outside the time-space continuum entirely, into a realm called "potential." In the terms in which we understand existence, the electron ceases to "exist."

Where does it go? Some physicists now describe a domain outside of space-time where all existence is potential, awaiting the influence of *conscious intention* to manifest. The electron drops out of space-time, into the realm of potential, and comes back when and where an observer looks for it. "Everything we know about Nature," the physicist Henry Stapp declares, "is in accord with the idea that the fundamental process of Nature lies outside space-time but generates events that can be located in space-time." By observing reality we enter into a relationship with it which changes whatever we are observing. Even though from our customary perspective, reality appears reliably stable and solid, all electrons everywhere are passing into and out of existence constantly. They pass out of time and space and reemerge only in response to the presence of conscious awareness.

Quantum physics offers us an astonishing message: consciousness seems to be a fundamental component of the construction of the universe. Nothing that happens is external to awareness! Just as space-time and matter-energy "inter-are," consciousness and reality "inter-are." Consciousness and existence are also a continuum.

If, as quantum physics suggests, every particle is at each moment consciously called from a unified domain of potential into existence, and particles of everything are interchanging constantly, then separateness is indeed the illusion and we are back to where we began!

This radical view is remarkably consonant with the Jewish mystics' claim: "All worlds, together with everything that is created, existed potentially within Infinite Being." As the Baal Shem Tov said: "Nothing other than God exists in all the universe. When you look at a physical thing, remember, you are looking at the immanent Divine Presence!" We have returned to what our *brakha* has wanted us to remember all along: Nothing is outside of God. And this is the ultimate mystery.

As Rav Kook proclaimed: "We cannot identify the abundant vitality within all living beings . . . nor the hidden vitality enfolded within inanimate creation. Everything constantly flows, vibrates, and aspires. Nor can we estimate our own inner abundance. Our inner world is sealed and concealed, linked to a hidden something, a world that is not our world. . . . Everything teems with richness, everything aspires to ascend and be purified. Everything sings, celebrates, serves, develops, evolves, uplifts, aspires to be arranged in oneness."

Mystics and God-seekers of all cultures and times have discovered this secret. "The ultimate meaning and purpose of life," offers Bede Griffiths, "cannot properly be thought. It is present everywhere, in everything, yet it always escapes our grasp. It is the 'Ground' of all existence, that from which all things come, to which all things return, but which never appears. It is 'within' all things, 'above' all things, 'beyond' all things, but it cannot be identified with anything. Without it nothing could exist, without it nothing could be known, yet it is itself unknown. It is that by which everything is known, yet which itself remains unknown. It is 'unseen but seeing, unheard but hearing, unperceived but perceiving, unknown but knowing.' . . . We speak of 'God' but this also is only a name for this inexpressible mystery."

This is the mystery of which the Indian mystic poet Kabir sings:

O how may I ever express that secret word?
O how can I say He is not like this,
and He is like that?
If I say that He is within me,

the universe is ashamed:
If I say He is without me
it is falsehood.
He makes the inner and outer worlds to be indivisibly one;
The conscious and the unconscious,
both are His footstools.
He is neither manifest nor hidden
He is neither revealed nor un-revealed.
There are no words to tell that which He is.

The medieval Christian mystic Meister Eckhart also bore witness
to this truth:

God created all things in such a way
that they are not outside of God's self
as ignorant people imagine.
Rather:
All creatures flow outward, but nonetheless remain
within God.
God created all things this way;
not that they might stand outside of
God, nor alongside God,
nor beyond God,
but that they might
come into God
and receive God
and dwell in God.

For this reason everything that is
is bathed in God,
is enveloped by God,
who is round-about us all, enveloping us.

Being is God's circle
and in this circle
all creatures exist.
Everything that is in God
is God.

The physicist explores the universe and says, "Nothing is outside of consciousness." I sing with the Psalmist: *"Adonay, You are the dwelling place!"*

In the *Olam* we discover that not only time-space, matter-energy, and you-I, but even consciousness and reality "inter-are." We and God "inter-are." This is the ultimate mystery: all reality is inside God and is God. In *Olam* at every moment every atom of us is being called from infinite potential into life.

In the beginning, there was existence alone.
One only—without a second.
It, the One, thought to itself:
Let Me be many.
Let Me grow forth.
Thus out of Itself
It projected the universe
And having projected the Universe out of Itself
It entered into every being.

All that is has its self in It alone.
Of all things It is the subtle essence.
It is truth.
It is the Self
And you are That.

—*Chandogya Upanishad*

∞

Then you gather everything,
Without hatred, jealousy, or rivalry.
The light of peace and a fierce boldness manifest in you.
The splendor of compassion,
And the glory of love shine through you.
The desire to act and work,
The passion to create and restore yourself,
The yearning for silence and for the inner shout of joy—
These all band together in your spirit,
And you become holy.

—RAV ABRAHAM ISAAC KOOK

My heart is ready!
O God, my heart is ready!

—PSALM 57:8

Concluding a *Brakha*

◈◈◈

A *brakha* is a two-part formula. The first six words—*Barukh Ata Adonay Eloheynu Melekh Ha'Olam*—make up the opening segment. Recall how we used the image of a stage to portray the function of these opening words of a *brakha:* the lights of the theater are dim, the crowd is waiting; as music begins, the curtains open and a spotlight comes on; a mood of expectancy fills the hall....

Once the curtains are up and the spotlight is on, there are so many expressions of appreciation we may place on the stage.

We begin:

בָּרוּךְ אַתָּה יהוה אֱלֹהֵינוּ מֶלֶךְ הָעוֹלָם...

Barukh Ata Adonay Eloheynu Melekh Ha'Olam....

and then can offer: *"borey pri ha'gafen,"* praising the Source of All for "creating the fruit of the vine" which we drink as wine or grape

141

juice; or *"ha'motzi lechem min ha'aretz,"* praising the Source for "bring-ing forth nourishing bread from the earth." There is an array of expressions of gratitude, drawn from tradition or our own hearts, which we can offer. With each *brakha* we reorient our lives toward holiness and participate in the flow of *shefa* into the world. With each *brakha* we stretch our souls to receive and attach ourselves to the ascending sparks of holiness our *brakha* releases.

Isaac Luria reminds us: "By saying a *brakha* before you enjoy something, your soul partakes spiritually. As the Torah states, 'One does not live on bread alone, but rather on all that issues from the mouth of God.' Not just the physical but the spiritual—the holy sparks springing from the mouth of God, like the soul herself, breathed into us by God. So when you eat, say the *motzi!* Then, by eating, you bring forth sparks that cleave to your soul." Says the Maggid: "Place all your thoughts into the power of your words until you see the light of the words. You can then see how one word shines into another, and how many lights are brought forth."

A Fountain of Blessings	ברוך	*Barukh*
are You!	אתה	*Ata*
The-Eternal-Breath-of-Life-Beyond-and-Within,	יהוה	*Adonay*
Divine Expansiveness Concentrated within our World	אלהנו	*Eloheynu*
Channeling Creative Power to Manifest as	מלך	*Melekh*
the Mystery of Consciousness becoming Time-Space	העולם	*Ha'Olam*

Through our *brakhot* our lives are enriched. Infused with holy energy, our souls arise to partake of the adventure of the universe. We bless the Source of Life and we are blessed.

—◦⟨⟩◦—

In the appendix you will find a compilation of some of the many *brakhot* Jewish tradition offers us, as well as an invitation to craft new *brakhot* of your own.

> For all of the wondrous moments of our lives
> we place our gratitude
> in the spotlight.

אשד קדשנו במצותו

Fix your mind on Me.
Give your heart's love to Me.
Consecrate all your actions to My service.
Hold yourself as nothing before me.
To Me then shall you come.
Truly I promise,
for you are dear to me.

—BHAGAVAD GITA

ברוך אתה יהוה אלהנו מלך העולם

Barukh Ata Adonay Eloheynu Melekh ha'Olam

אשר קדשנו במצותו וציונו . . .

asher kid'shanu b'mitzvotav, v'tzivanu . . .

A Fountain of Blessings are You
The-Eternal-Breath-of-Life-Beyond-and-Within,
Divine Expansiveness Concentrated within our World,
Channeling Creative Power to Manifest as
the Mystery of Consciousness becoming Time-Space
Who makes us holy through mitzvot and commands us. . . .

Using a *Brakha* to Introduce a *Mitzvah*

෨෨෪෨෨

Thus far we have spoken about the role of a *brakha* as a spiritual practice of appreciation and praise. A *brakha* can also be an expression of our intention to perform a sacred act. Using a *brakha* in this way, we announce our intention to become actors on the stage by engaging in the practice of *mitzvot* (plural form). A *mitzvah* can be thought of as a spiritual "action-directive" designed to sustain or repair the flow of God-energy through

Creation, to enhance the realm of the sacred, and promote *kedusha*. Blessing itself is one such *mitzvah*.

A *mitzvah* is an action deriving from our realization that our God-awareness itself makes demands upon us. Entering into an intimate relationship with God means entering into relationship with a Presence calling us not only to be but also to do. In order to fulfill our purpose, our awareness of divinity must flow from consciousness into action.

When we use a *brakha* in this way, it is the tradition to follow the opening words with this phrase: אשר קדשנו במצותו וציונו *asher kid'shanu b'mitzvotav v'tzivanu*... We praise God as the One Power who has sanctified us with *mitzvot* and has commanded us to fulfill a specific sacred act. "Sanctify" enters English from the Latin *sanctificare*, meaning "to make sacred." *Sanctus*—"holy" or "sacred," *facere*—"to make." Using Hebrew we could say, to become *kadosh*. The words of this portion of the *brakha* recognize God as "the One who *kid'sh-* (makes-sacred) *-anu* (us)," the One who makes it possible for us to become *kadosh*. How? *"b'mitzvotav,"* through the sacred actions called *mitzvot*. With these words we call out to the Holy One as the Source who directs us toward holiness. Out of our relationship with God comes the imperative to live sacred lives through sacred action.

What are these sacred actions called *mitzvot*? How can *mitzvot* help us become *kadosh* and realize our sacred potential?

מצוה *Mitzvah*

What is a *mitzvah*?

The word *mitzvah* is often translated as "commandment," or, more colloquially, "good deed." For many of us, *mitzvah* as "good deed" conveys warm associations (who wouldn't want to do a good deed?), but as "commandment" it seems like a laundry list of repressive restrictions.

In rejecting Orthodoxy, most Jews have abandoned the path of obligatory *mitzvot* as hopelessly enmeshed in coercive social systems of the past. No longer understanding themselves as "commanded" by a "Commander," many Jews see the term as valuable only in its generic association with vaguely beneficial behavior or customs.

Yet *mitzvah* is too potent a word to rest easy with this diminution. At its center lie the root letters צ *tzadi* and ו *waw* as צו *TzV* (as in *miTzVotav* and *v'TziVanu*). These letters reach toward us with a compelling message. *Tzadi* is a letter which suggests the consolidation of energy and the building of structure. It conveys the sense of constructive or right action (as in the word *tzaddik*, a righteous or holy person). *Waw*, as we saw in the chapter on *aleph*, is a reaching-out letter, extending, linking and conjoining. We can think of the letters צו *TzV* as instructing us: Organize your energy and project it into the world! Give structure to what you know and make it manifest!

These letters can help us renew our understanding of *mitzvot* as actions organizing our energy in God-directed ways. The notion of *mitzvot* requires us to translate our recognition of the One within Creation and within ourselves into a commitment to behavior manifesting Godliness. The call to take on *mitzvot* is a call to make a sustained commitment though our own actions to practices revealing the divinity in all Creation.

—❦—

Through Torah we have heard the divine voice speak to us saying, "Be *kadosh*, sacred beings, because I am *kadosh*, because I am sacred," urging us to consider all our actions—however mundane—as opportunities to manifest the sacred potential of each moment. We are asked to expand and enhance our connection with the divine with every motion of our lives.

This may not seem easy! There are many pressures in our daily lives, and we can so easily be caught up in patterns of behavior thwarting our desire to be holy in the world. In a materialistic culture even our spiritual yearnings can be commercialized as consumer fads serving highly privatized ego needs, divorced from community or any sense of social obligation.

Yet we know that the rich and purposeful life we long for is not achieved by distancing ourselves from others to seek personal fulfillment or enlightenment, or by neglecting the ongoing struggles of life to pursue the latest spiritual fashion. We want genuine connection, real community, and real lives. We want clarity of purpose and hope to find a deep inner radiance that can suffuse all our tasks and relationships.

The practice of *mitzvot* is a path toward this possibility. Like the adjustments offered by a chiropractor or the regular practice of yoga postures keeping the vertebrae and body in healthy alignment, *mitzvot* are subtle exercises to keep the soul flexible and healthy so our lives can be rich and purposeful.

Peak experiences give us glimpses of clarity and insight, but sustained practice brings them into every facet of our daily lives Says Rabbi Levi Yitzhak of Berdichev: "There is no greater path than this. For wherever you go and whatever you do—even mundane activities—you serve God."

By our practice we take moments of wonder and exhilaration and blend them into the rhythms of our days. Reb Zalman has called this "domesticating the peak experience." To domesticate means to bring into my domicile, into the place where I live. When I bring my most expanded consciousness into my everyday life, I discover that my whole life can be a sacred endeavor. Spirituality cannot be purchased; the sacred life must be lived. Happily, the regular practice of *mitzvot* is not all that hard, for the divine light shines within each moment. Our task in every detail of life is to make that light manifest.

—⚭—

The mindful actions we undertake as *mitzvot* balance each other, touching all parts of our being. Our bodies and psyches hold many-layered memories, habits, physical and emotional reflexes, instincts, patterns of responses, ways of knowing, and ways of being. We have centers of awareness of which we are barely conscious and noncognitive ways of learning that are difficult even to articulate. Educators are only just beginning to acknowledge the nonverbal intelligence expressed in sensory, emotional, intuitive, or physical capabilities.

The system of *mitzvot* embodies this understanding that diverse centers of awareness must be activated for full learning to take place. There are *mitzvot* that touch us on different levels and speak to varied aspects of our being. The system of *mitzvot* reflects profound respect for the complexity of the human body and psyche, addressing us by the many different textures and flavors of our awareness. There are *mitzvot* that are easy to explain cognitively, and there are *mitzvot* for which intuition offers only subtle hints of a power we do not fully grasp. There are *mitzvot* of "doing" and *mitzvot* of "refraining from doing." There are *mitzvot* that involve ritual, while others are clearly ethical. Some focus directly on our relationship with God; others more directly address our relationships with one another. Some are deeply personal, others communal, while yet others stress the sacred dimension of our relationship with the earth.

Mitzvot sometimes unfold their benefits only subtly and gradually. The growth of a tree, year by year, is barely noticeable. We walk in the redwood forest and gaze in awe at these ancient giants. They stood when Columbus sailed, when the Declaration of Independence was signed, when we were born. We are humbled by the enormity of the slow accretion of growth. The trees around us are growing even now and we cannot see it.

So also do we grow with *mitzvot*. With many—such as *tzedakah* correcting economic injustice, *bikkur cholim* visiting the sick, or *bal tashchit* not being wasteful—we can understand clearly how we progress. *V'ahavta l'rayakha kamokha*, the *mitzvah* "Love your fellow person as yourself," is the basis of our practice of offering loving compassion toward all our companions and associates, including those who we find less easy to like. The *mitzvah tza'ar baaley chayyim* forbids causing pain to any living creature and is a feature of the *mitzvot* of *kashrut*, sacred principles for eating.

V'shinantam l'vanekha, requiring us to teach love of God and Torah to our children, supports bedtime rituals for little ones, and other family time, as well as ongoing religious education. *L'kadesh et Yom Ha'Shabbat*, the *mitzvah* of making Shabbos a sacred experience, offers time out from the work world for vital personal, family, and communal "soul" time. *V'samachta b'chagekha* offers us festivals of rejoicing linking our lives to the natural cycles of earth, sun, and moon, and to the cycles of myth and history, giving context to our spiritual journeys.

In practice, even though we may be incorporating scores of *mitzvot* into the fabric of our days, a *brakha* is usually offered only as part of a *mitzvah* involving action. Among these are the *mitzvah* of studying Torah; the *mitzvah* of lighting the candles for Shabbos, festivals, and the nights of Chanukah; the *mitzvah* of dedicating our hands to sacred purpose while washing in preparation for eating bread; the *mitzvah* of wearing a garment with *tzitzit* (the macramé fringes tied on the four corners of a *tallis* to remind us of the presence of God and our commitment to the *mitzvot*); the *mitzvah* of wearing *t'fillin* (the leather armband and headband housing scrolls of Torah passages); the *mitzvah* of *mezuzzah* (affixing to the doors of our homes a parchment scroll containing the *Shema* and Torah passages reminding us of the *mitzvot* of comprehending the Unity of God and returning God's love with our own); and the *mitzvah* of immersion in the rebirthing waters of the *mikvah*.

Through our *mitzvot* we express our desire to repair all that is damaged and broken in this world and in realms even beyond our imperfect understanding. Each time we undertake a *mitzvah*, we create a shift in ourselves and the universe that eases the way for the next *mitzvah* and then the next. With each *mitzvah* we affirm that we live consciously within the flow of God and intend each of our actions to be yet another window into the fullness of the Divine Presence.

Mitzvot as Spiritual Imperatives

Jewish tradition teaches that none are exempt from the practice of *mitzvot*. Not even a *tzaddik*, an enlightened or fully righteous one, may say, "I am a fully realized person. I've reached the goal and certainly no longer need 'practice.' That's for the novices!" No matter where we are on the path, we all still need *mitzvot* in our lives.

The *mitzvah* of *tzedakah*, for example, requiring that we each allocate a percentage of our income as direct contributions to correct economic injustice, can certainly be thought of as a "good deed." It is truly good to give to others, good to give food to the hungry or money to the poor. But when undertaken as a *mitzvah* this giving assumes another dimension. The practices we take on as *mitzvot* are more than casual personal choices; they are spiritual imperatives. As Jews we experience ourselves as collectively obligated to certain behavior because of the compelling nature of our experience of God. Jewish tradition has high praise for one who holds this sense of obligation as taking precedence over individual freedom of choice. Choosing is good, but the poor, Jewish teaching points out, should not have to wait for their *tzedakah* until the rich "choose" to give.

Giving is therefore not volitional charity. So strong is the sense of obligation that the *mitzvah* of *tzedakah* is incumbent on all, not only the affluent. In fact, the only person Jewish tradition exempts from the *mitzvah* of *tzedakah* is one who literally does not know where the next meal is coming from. If I have only my daily sandwich, *tzedakah* obligates me to share it with someone who has none.

I share it, even if at that moment I don't feel like it, because my relationship with God requires this of me.

In a curious twist the *mitzvah* of *tzedakah*, one of the most significant of the action-*mitzvot*, is undertaken without a *brakha*. The explanation? Not even a delay as brief as a *brakha* should impede the imperative to give.

In contemporary America, however, religious practice is essentially volitional. There is no coercion; spiritual expression is a personal choice. What can it mean to declare that for us *mitzvot* are spiritual imperatives?

A well-known sociologist once recounted to me his experience in an Orthodox rabbinical *yeshiva*, in which he asked the students how many of them chose to be obligated to the *mitzvot*. When they all raised their hands, he said, "You choose to be obligated? Had I asked you this question a hundred years ago, not one hand would have gone up!" To be obligated is, after all, to have no choice. In the past, when individuals were bound by social and conceptual constraints within the tradition and status of their birth, obligations to family, community, state, and God were fixed and enforced. A wholly externalized Divine Authority matched the feudal hierarchies of society. God "ruled" through command, and the loyal folk obeyed.

Today, few of us still retain a view of God as a King "up there" literally dictating minutiae of human behavior. And still the power of *mitzvot* derives in significant measure from their very nature as incumbent upon us, as compelling. Where, then, is the locus of the imperative once there is no commander, no coercion, once I can choose or relinquish obligations as I wish?

Connection and Covenant

Torah singles out two archetypal personalities, Noah and Avraham, for praise in an unusual way. Although one is a Jew, one not, they share a common distinction. They are each praised in Torah as *tam*, without guile, and as *tzaddik*, righteous; of each it is said that he walks facing God. Each faces God in a way that brings God and humans into a *covenantal* relationship.

When we walk through our lives facing God in openness, without pretense, and fully present to the sacred dimension of each moment, marvelous possibilities open up to us. When we align our lives with godly desires, we become like Noah and Avraham: "God-walkers." We feel ourselves called to live in the light of our discovery that the One Source wants us, loves us, fills us. We step forward to stand in that light like a lover coming to the *chuppah*, the wedding canopy where love becomes commitment. In Jewish tradition, commitment is called *brit*, "covenant." We discover, as did Noah and Avraham, that we are called to live every moment in conscious relationship with the One. We enter into covenant.

The covenants undertaken by Noah and Avraham established that we and God are eternally entwined in a bond of mutual responsibility. The covenant of Noah embraces all humanity, the whole earth and all its creatures. Our ancestor Avraham, with his partner Sarah, initiated the unique Jewish relationship with God that would eventually bring our people to the momentous collective epiphany of Sinai and to an eternal commitment to bear witness to the divine unity through Torah and *mitzvot*. Thus Noah and Avraham begin the God-walk that leads to Sinai.

It is the custom to spend the night of Shavuot, the festival cel-ebrating the Revelation at Sinai and our receiving the Torah, singing and learning together throughout the night. At dawn, wrapped in *tallesim*, we *davven* Shacharit, pray the morning prayers, and chant Torah, as the sun rises. Each year at Shavuot we gather to "stand again at Sinai." The point of the gathering, however, is more than a ritual commemoration, more even than a reenactment. It is, in intent, an opportunity, through the intensity of shared story, song, and teaching, for each of us to experience revelation personally, for each of us to hear God's voice anew, speaking to us in a transformative way.

One year in my community we began our gathering just as evening was falling, by marching seven times around the perimeter of the property—one cycle for each of the seven weeks our people spent in the wilderness, on our way to Sinai—before entering the house, where we tied rainbow *tzitzit* on a sparking white-and-gold *tallis.* We raised the *tallis* high on *chuppah* poles, and sang, danced, and learned Torah under that wedding canopy far into the night. Such is the magic of Sinai.

At Sinai we enter into a deeper reality beyond space and time. Walls of separation break down and we step into the Is-ness of God. The revelation at Sinai described in *midrash* is a moment of time-less now. Here at Sinai, the river of linear time halts. Time stops. History ceases. Eternity pierces Creation. At Sinai, God and world fuse and the hidden light is revealed. Midrashic legend tells us that every Jewish soul who would ever be born into (or would ever seek out) the Jewish path in any lifetime was present at Sinai. Enveloped by eternity, each soul received Torah, washed in the soundless reverberations of the silent *Aleph* of the Divine "I AM."

To "stand at Sinai" is to stand timelessly within God. Perhaps it is not by accident that reaching Sinai requires us to travel a considerable distance in the wilderness. Jewish sources often play with a Hebrew pun linking the word for "wilderness," *midbar*, with the word for "speaking" *m'daber*. It is not that we lack the natural capacity to hear God's voice speaking at every moment. It is just that we are usually unavailable. Our lives are too cluttered, too busy, too filled with the noise of our old habits and assumptions. The path to God's voice takes us through the naked terrain of not-knowing in which everything is risked and everything inessential is stripped away.

The *midrash* tells us that all who experienced revelation at Sinai heard with their eyes and saw with their ears in a fusion of senses overtaking the whole body. But neither hearing, seeing, nor feeling fully describes what is happening. Inner and outer voices blend in a full-body knowing melding all the senses in a singular epiphany. When God's voice is heard, the body knows from its core, from the inside out rather than from the outside in.

Torah tells us that at Sinai, when Moshe spoke to God, God answered him, *"b'kol,"* "with sound" or perhaps even "with voice." The rabbis ask, "With voice? With sound? With what voice, what sound?" What was the God "sound/voice" Moshe heard? They respond with an extraordinary teaching. Moshe, they say, heard God speak *"b'kolo shel Moshe,"* with Moshe's own voice! He heard God's voice as his own voice. He heard from the inside out!

The Living God speaks to each of us from the inside out, in our own voice. For my soul to recognize God's voice there must be an inner voice I hear, an imperative in the depths of my soul. The word "commandment" casts God's voice as if it were only a voice of external authority, but our teachers know that when we truly hear, we hear an inner voice and touch an inner knowing as well. Or perhaps we should say that when we hear God's voice, outside and inside merge to become the same place. The voice of God addresses us from within and from without at the same time!

This is the authentic voice that speaks to us in the crystalline moments of our lives. I would like to challenge us to dive deeply enough into life, into Torah, and into committed spiritual practice to encounter not merely authority but authenticity. We will know we are compelled to sacred action when we have learned to hear the "voice that is both within and without" simultaneously as God's voice and our own. Then we will respond to the call to live sacred lives because this call resonates with our very being.

Obligation and Sacred Relationship

There is a kind of knowing that becomes possible only in intimacy. When we transcend our separateness and enter into "I-Thouness," a boundary is crossed, a threshold passed over, and change occurs for both the "I" and the "Thou." Then we are no longer "beings" but rather "becomings," like the God of the Burning Bush, who is *Ehyeh Asher Ehyeh*, the I-Am-Becoming of the universe. Each of us is an interdependent becoming—inter-active, inter-existent with each other self.

At such times of I-Thou awareness, not only the awareness but also consequences shift. When I open myself to the "thou" of you, I must live in the knowing that has passed between us. I may no longer behave in a way denying what we share. My integrity is remolded in relationship. Perhaps those moments when we grasp the full extent of our inter-being can be thought of as our Sinai moments. Then we understand each *mitzvah* as a medium through which we can re-live that moment of eternity stored in our once-and-future memory of Sinai, where spirit and matter, God, world, and we are One.

A *mitzvah* is an action that commands us because it derives from our experience of the infinite. Through each *mitzvah* a window opens. Past, present, and future meld again to become a unitive now. In our ultimate moments of inter-being, Infinite God and finite "we" meet. We embrace the sacred dimension and "inter-are." Each *mitzvah* reopens a window of aliveness to our life within God. We are capable of reawakening our memory of standing within God, but without a cohesive spiritual practice, our remembrance will be erratic and fleeting.

Moments of inter-being are sometimes called experiences of *Atzilut:* the interpenetration of life-force in commingling essence. Recall the teaching of the *Zohar* that love, which begins with physical attraction, leads to communication and then to the awareness of breath culminating in a kiss. At the moment of the kiss, lovers share each other's life-force. This progression toward ever-greater intimacy also evolves in our relationship with God. *Atzilut,* "the kiss," describes a most intimate sharing between self and God. Experiences of *Atzilut* change our lives, even change history.

As lovers reshape their behavior in order to increase the frequency of moments revealing their love to each other, so we as a people can reshape our behavior in order that we return again and again to the exhilaration of our inter-being with God. In each of those moments we return to savor the glow, bliss, and liberation of God's love. Each time we make love with God, we stand at Sinai in *Atzilut,* in that timeless kiss of shared being.

I would like to do a *mitzvah* like a lover running to fall into the embrace of her beloved. In that kiss I lose myself and find myself. In that kiss I swear that no action of mine will ever betray our love. In that kiss my soul's radiance wants to shine from one end of Creation to the other and make every moment of my being a testimony that heaven and earth can touch and eternity be seen.

Ah, but . . .

In the learning and teaching I have shared in the Quaker community, I have often heard the sense of obligation described as "feeling the weight" of a concern. In Hebrew the word for weight is *kavod,* which is also used to mean the Glory or Presence of God. We "feel the weight" when we feel ourselves saturated with the living Presence of God. We "feel the weight" because the living Presence is pushing upon us and within us.

But the notion of *mitzvot* being obligatory is problematic as well as exciting. What do we do when we encounter a *mitzvah* we don't understand, or that we think we do understand and therefore reject? Is the system fixed and sealed, or is it flexible and unfolding? Is it ancient wisdom or ancient prejudices? Is the authority to craft the *mitzvot* allocated only to a hierarchy of male legalists in a particular chain of rabbinic command, or can we approach the evolution of *mitzvot* in a feminist, historical, and critical way? Do we practice only the things we understand and appreciate? Can we understand and appreciate without practice?

I once was counseling a couple learning Jewish spiritual practice and working out issues in their relationship. They regularly fought about money, and we spoke about how money becomes a metaphor for conflict. We also worked on a budget. One week, when we had learned about lighting candles and making Shabbos, I suddenly told them that I wanted them to allocate a reasonable but not inconsiderable sum for *tzedakah*, before they lit Shabbos candles each week.

Now these were people who said that they had to struggle to pay my modest fee and could barely cover their other bills. I don't know how I had the gall to give them this assignment; I felt almost as if a voice was coming through me. I still wonder why they didn't just walk out—but they agreed.

As time went by, I noticed I wasn't talking to them about money any more. Then, several months later, they told me how my assignment had turned their entire lives around. They said that being obligated to be givers freed them from the tyranny of thinking of themselves as poor. Suddenly they became philanthropists. As their view shifted, they discovered they not only had enough but they had become rich in their own eyes. They spent less and stopped arguing about money. I learned a lesson. Had *tzedakah* been voluntary, had I said to them, write out a check when you are so inclined, this magic would never have happened.

For over a century *mikvah*, the ritual bath, was not seen by modern Jews as a valuable *mitzvah*. To liberal Jews, the ancient practice requiring married women to immerse themselves in the waters of the *mikvah* prior to resuming marital relations after menstruation, was dismissed as implying that women's bodies were unclean. Modern hygiene and more enlightened viewpoints clearly made this superstitious ritual passé.

Yet in recent years, Jewish feminists have begun to reclaim this ancient practice. We have come to understand more about the role water plays in the subconscious, its connection to womb and birth, and some say even to evolutionary memories of our amphibious origins, deeply embedded in the human brainstem.

As we immerse ourselves naked in the warm *mikvah* water of our Mother's womb, in the *mayim chayyim*, the living waters of the Divine Presence, we can let go of all the hurts and disappointments, all the unfulfilled promises of the past, and be open once again to the original blessing that is ours without asking. Just as in the womb there are no judgments, no critiques, in the *mikvah* we reclaim the purity of our souls, bathed in love. When ready, we emerge from the waters prepared to take our lives up with renewed hope and understanding. That part of our brain remembering birth experiences the living waters of the *mikvah* as an aid to our own rebirthing. We begin to understand why the *mitzvah* requires us to immerse ourselves in water physically, not just in the idea. The concept alone will not transform us.

Mikvah has been reclaimed as a powerful tool for transformation and healing. How tragic it would have been had everyone abandoned *mikvahs* in years past, for then there would have been none for us to rediscover.

—⚬❦⚬—

Yet in spite of all the good we discern, there are also *mitzvot* "on the books" that autocratically exclude women, that punish gays; *mitzvot* whose interpretation has historically been the prerogative of an exclusively male chain of authority absorbed in and reflecting all the wounding oppressions and misogynistic attitudes of earlier times; *mitzvot* whose enactment has been encrusted by so many layers of repressive rules and restrictions that the light within is hard to see.

Nor can the practice of *mitzvot,* or any other spiritual practice, overcome every trauma or prevent all evil behavior. As the daily newspapers attest, there are wounds of psyche and spirit harsh enough to put spirituality itself in the service of violence and rage. Religious systems globally do not lack for teachings that systematically demonize enemies, legitimize violence, and degrade and demean women and outsiders.

So, what can we do?

The rabbis who reconstructed Jewish life after the destruction of the *Beyt Ha'Mikdash,* the Second Temple, were the midwives of a paradigm shift which initiated halakhic Judaism, a Judaism based on Torah and *mitzvot* as interpreted by rabbinic authority. Halakhic Jews assume unquestioningly the eternal validity of that chain of command and assign authority for its evolution only to rabbis trained in Jewish law, historically an exclusively male elite. Non-halakhic Jews have abandoned the premise that the full package of traditional Jewish practice is binding, and participate in flexibly interpreted Jewish customs. Thus for most Jews outside the Orthodox minority, *halakha* is no longer the context of their lives.

History is change. Out of nomadic biblical Judaism evolved the complex sacred practice of the Temple, itself transformed in turn into halakhic Judaism by the revolutionary vision of the rabbis. Then medieval feudalism gave way to modernity in a vast economic and conceptual upheaval replacing land-based agrarian economies and their rigid social hierarchies with capitalism, the democratic "social contract," and unprecedented technological growth. The success of each paradigm fostered the growth of the very phenomena that both built upon and replaced it.

History is now moving us toward the next shift—not, I hope, toward a minimalist and purely personal "non-halakhic" Judaism but toward a "post-halakhic" Judaism deeply rooted in the contributions of the rabbinic paradigm but "reformatted" to take Jewish wisdom, spiritual insight, and committed practice into the next age.

We are as a human community moving (however fitfully) into an era that will reshape the whole human story. Out of the ashes of the most terrible man-made destructions human history has known, a new view of the earth and our role in its evolution is emerging. Old forms, old "reality maps," however tenacious, are slowly giving way in the face of unprecedented forces of change.

The planet shrinks as global communications and computer technologies link individuals and cultures in patterns of interconnection unimaginable a few short years ago. Science, which once strove to demystify nature, now points us again to the fundamental mystery of all existence. Feminism encourages women's voices toward full participation in the human community, supporting global movements to bring women full human rights and honor women's wisdom. A radically new ecological awareness comprehends the inherent connectedness of all the fragile ecosystems of our planet. Human-potential movements expand our capacities for growth and illuminate new horizons for human aspirations. An egalitarian, humanistic consciousness spreads, rejecting all forms of abusive power and celebrating the intrinsic worth of each human being. Space exploration pushes our minds to imagine and embrace our planetary citizenship. In both a perilous and a tremendously exciting time of human history, a new metamorphosis begins.

Jewish renewal is a response to the desire to tap ancient wisdom in the service of the future. We are creating an authentic and inspired Jewish life-style, which applies Jewish spiritual teaching to the array of new concerns facing the human community. We embrace a vision of renewal that updates and restores the Jewish mystical tradition to centrality, and brings the richness of Jewish meditation back into the mainstream of Jewish spiritual practice. Hasidic teaching brings us a rich legacy of insight into the psychospiritual dimension of prayer and a path of joyous celebration fostering enriched personal and communal spiritual practice. We affirm that legacy and employ it to nurture the spiritual journey of each unique person and honor the truths expressed in all faith traditions.

The path that began with Sarah our mother and Avraham our father unfolds and continues to offer its wisdom and guidance, bringing new meanings to ancient *mitzvot.* Torah warns us that our species' capacity to dominate the earth and all life must be channeled for good. The *mitzvot* of *kashrut,* for example, empower us to ask, "Is Styrofoam kosher? What about hormonal and chemical food additives? What could a spiritually informed relationship to food look like in this culture?" The *mitzvah* of *tza'ar baaley chayyim* impels us to ask, "Shouldn't raising animals in cruel animal factories be forbidden?" *Bal tashchit,* "do not waste," informs our efforts to recycle and our struggle to keep our planet's threatened ecosystems alive. The *mitzvah* of Shabbos compels us to seek the restructuring of our society's relationship to work and to rest, so we can collectively reassess the meaning of productivity and best discern how the productive capacities of our working people should be directed.

An Evolving Path

Mitzvot as a spiritual system is evolving, not fixed. It is the mixed product of our people's best listening to God speaking within us and around us, through sacred texts and sacred lives, in good times and bad. In each generation we listen and understand as best we can. I am a newcomer to this endeavor, and I honor the depth and complexity of the work that came before. I do not feel free to reject it lightly. At the same time, I don't want to abrogate my right to join in, to be part of evolution.

We have inherited a profound spiritual and ethical path, but not a completed one. That itself is a great gift. One of the ironies of Jewish-Christian dialogue is that Christianity is often described as the religion of grace and Judaism portrayed, somewhat pejoratively, as a religion of "law." The irony is that the gift of Sinai and Torah is understood in Jewish tradition as the ultimate act of grace. Yet even Torah is called by the *Zohar* "an unripe fruit of Divine wisdom." It is we who participate in the ripening.

When I say *asher kid'shanu b'mitzvotav,* I praise God as the Power who makes it possible for us to strive for *kedusha,* aided by the gift of an array of extraordinary spiritual practices. But *mitzvot* are not merely a fixed collection of rules to follow mindlessly, and *v'tzivanu* means more than "and has commanded us." God as the Voice-both-beyond-and-within has enabled us, invited us, illuminated for us, a path, a way of uplifting ourselves and realizing our divinity. The path toward holiness is holy just to walk.

Letting God In

Once the Kotzker Rebbe posed the same question to his students that my husband asked the children in the *sukkah:* "Where is God?" The children all pointed toward the sky. At an adult spiritual retreat some participants pointed at their hearts, others pointed in a circle all around them. The Kotzker Rebbe's answer was a simple one: "God is where we let God in."

In the very first question in Torah God calls out to the earth-ling, "Where are you?" We let God in when we turn to face God and find God turning to face us calling, "Where are you?" Like Avraham and generations of others, we call out *Hineni,* "Here I am." Here I am, ready and prepared. Here, I am present and open. I wear no mask. I am free of pretense. Here I am with all that I can offer, which is my life. What is it You would have me do?

At such a moment we again enter the covenant; we are lovers, accountable not only for our intentions but for our actions. Awareness without action is like a love unconsummated. At those moments when we and God turn to face each other in fully mutual "I-Thou-ness," we grasp our role as finite beings with Godly work to do. We are partners with God in perfecting Creation or even, as one radical commentary suggests, as partners in the fulfillment and perfection of God. We pray that our actions will be an extension of the light of God, a channel for divine intention, true and faithful to the mutuality of our desire.

When I call out my *brakha* to the Source of life, I open myself again to the Wholeness. I am recognized and loved. In the intimacy of connection I feel not only an embrace but also a demand, an enveloping and unfolding imperative to act in alignment with the Whole. The Power that opens to me wants not only my praise but also my effort. Each *mitzvah* opens me again to that authentic within-and-without voice calling me to hope, love, praise, and act.

We are human beings whose souls are a spark of the living God whose Name is I AM. We are also human "doings" whose work is to reflect the divine character of the spark. Where is God? Living with us in holy relationship, flowing through us in holy intention, fulfilled in the covenant binding us to holy action.

> If your works are to live
> then God must move you
> from the inside—
> from the innermost regions
> of the soul.
>
> —MEISTER ECKHART

> To be in alignment with You
> is my desire
> For your Torah is within me.
>
> —PSALM 40:9

∞

Every vision born of earth is fleeting.
Every vision born of heaven is a blessing.
For people, the sight of spring warms their hearts.
For fish, the rhythm of the ocean is a blessing.
The brilliant sun that shines in every heart.
For the heaven's earth and all creatures.
What a blessing! . . .
The heart can't wait to speak of this ecstasy.
The soul is kissing the earth, saying
Oh God, what a blessing. . . .

—RUMI

If the only prayer
you say in your entire life
is "Thank You,"
that would suffice.

—MEISTER ECKHART

Appendix
Brakhot for Various Occasions

❦

I. *Brakhot* of Enjoyment, Praise, and Gratitude

בָּרוּךְ אַתָּה יהוה אֱלֹהֵנוּ מֶלֶךְ הָעוֹלָם...

Barukh Ata Adonay Eloheynu Melekh Ha'Olam . . .

For Food and Drink
I. The "all-purpose" *brakha* ("*shehakol*"):

The practice of making a *brakha* asks us to be aware of the nature and source of the food we are eating or the sensation we are appreciating. Offering the most accurate and specific *brakha* possible can be compared to sending a thank-you note that says "Dear Aunt Sophie, Thanks for the exotic hand-woven purple sweater from Mexico," as opposed to a generic card saying only "Thanks for your present." The *brakha* known as "*shehakol*" is the generic "thank-you card." It is an inclusive all-purpose *brakha*, appropriate for many individual foods (particularly those which do not grow from the earth) and also if one is uncertain which more specific *brakha* to use. (There are many books and pamphlets available at Jewish bookstores which can help you choose the most effective *brakha* for a wide range of foods.)

...שֶׁהַכֹּל נִהְיֶה בִּדְבָרוֹ.

... shehakol nih'yeh bid'varo: through whose word everything exists.

2. For bread *("ha'motzi")*:

...הַמּוֹצִיא לֶחֶם מִן הָאָרֶץ.

... ha'motzi lechem min ha'aretz: who brings forth bread from the earth.

3. For baked snack foods and other non-bread dough products:

...בּוֹרֵא מִינֵי מְזוֹנוֹת.

... borey miney mezonot: who creates all kinds of nourishment.

4. For grape wine:

...בּוֹרֵא פְּרִי הַגָּפֶן.

... borey pri ha'gafen: who creates the fruit of the vine.

5. For fruit which grows on trees:

...בּוֹרֵא פְּרִי הָעֵץ.

... borey pri ha'etz: who creates the fruit of the tree.

6. For a fruit or vegetable which grows directly from the earth:

...בּוֹרֵא פְּרִי הָאֲדָמָה.

... borey pri ha'adamah: who creates the fruit of the earth.

For Fragrances

I. For perfume or fragrant spices:

...בּוֹרֵא מִינֵי בְשָׂמִים.

... borey miney v'sammim: who creates all kinds of fragrant spices.

2. For fragrant shrubs or trees, or their flowers:

‎...בּוֹרֵא עֲצֵי בְשָׂמִים.

... borey atzey v'sammim: who creates fragrant trees.

3. For fragrant herbs, grasses, or flowers:

‎...בּוֹרֵא עִשְׂבֵי בְשָׂמִים.

... borey isvey v'sammim: who creates fragrant growing things.

4. For fragrant edible fruits or nuts:

‎...הַנּוֹתֵן רֵיחַ טוֹב בַּפֵּרוֹת.

... ha'noteyn reyach tov ba'peyrot: who imparts a good scent to fruits.

For Seeing Special Sights

I. For beauty in the natural world: people, animals, trees, fields ... :

‎...שֶׁכָּכָה לוֹ בָּעוֹלָמוֹ.

... sheh'kakhah lo ba'olamo: who has such as this in the universe!

2. For lightning, or natural wonders like a comet, majestic mountains, great rivers ... :

‎...עֹשֶׂה מַעֲשֵׂה בְרֵאשִׁית.

... oseh ma'asey v'reishit: who does the work of Creation (literally, who makes the making of "in-the-beginning.")

3. For seeing a rainbow in the sky:

‎...זוֹכֵר הַבְּרִית, וְנֶאֱמָן בִּבְרִיתוֹ, וְקַיָּם בְּמַאֲמָרוֹ.

... zokheyr ha'brit, v'neh'ehman biv'rito, v'kayam b'maamaro: who remembers and is faithful to the covenant.

4. For the sea:

‎...שֶׁעָשָׂה אֶת הַיָּם הַגָּדוֹל.

... sheh'asah et ha'yam ha'gadol: who made the great sea.

5. **For exceptionally strange-looking people or animals:**

...מְשַׁנֶּה הַבְּרִיּוֹת.

... *m'shaneh ha'briyot:* who makes varied creatures.

6. **For the first time you see a fruit tree bloom in the spring:**

...שֶׁלֹּא חִסַּר בָּעוֹלָמוֹ דָּבָר, וּבָרָא בוֹ בְּרִיּוֹת טוֹבוֹת
וְאִילָנוֹת טוֹבִים, לְהַנּוֹת בָּהֶם בְּנֵי אָדָם.

... *sheh'lo chisar ba'olamo davar, u'vara vo briyot tovot v'ilanot tovim, l'hanot ba'hem b'ney adam:* for a universe that lacks nothing, for [God] created in it good creatures and good trees so humans might enjoy them.

7. **Upon seeing a great Torah scholar:**

...שֶׁחָלַק מֵחָכְמָתוֹ לִירֵאָיו.

... *sheh'chalak mey'chokhmato li'rey'av:* who has given a share of Godly wisdom to the reverent.

8. **Upon seeing a great secular scholar:**

...שֶׁנָּתַן מֵחָכְמָתוֹ לְבָשָׂר וָדָם.

... *sheh-natan mey'chokhmato l'vasar vadam:* who has imparted Godly wisdom to human beings.

For Hearing

I. **Upon hearing thunder:**

...שֶׁכֹּחוֹ וּגְבוּרָתוֹ מָלֵא עוֹלָם.

... *sheh'kocho u'gevurato maley olam:* whose strength and power fill the universe.

2. **Upon hearing good news:**

...הַטּוֹב וְהַמֵּטִיב.

... *ha'tov v'ha'meytiv:* who is good and does good.

3. Upon hearing unusually bad news:

‎...דַּיַּן הָאֱמֶת.

. . . *dayan ha'emet:* the true Judge.

Other Brakhot *of Gratitude*

I. A *brakha* for "firsts" (*"sheh'hecheyanu"*), celebrating the first time in the cycle of a year, or in one's life that a special event occurs.

This special *brakha* helps us celebrate new experiences. Use it when eating a new seasonal fruit for the first time in the year (like a first ripe spring strawberry), or doing a seasonal *mitzvah* for the first time (such as lighting the first Chanukah candle), or for a birthday, an anniversary, a special vacation, or significant first experience of any appropriate kind.

‎...שֶׁהֶחֱיָנוּ וְקִיְּמָנוּ וְהִגִּיעָנוּ לַזְּמַן הַזֶּה.

. . . *sheh'hecheyanu, v'kiy'manu, v'higiyanu la'zman ha'zeh:* who has kept us alive, sustained us, and brought us to this time.

II. *Brakhot* for *Mitzvot*

‎בָּרוּךְ אַתָּה יהוה אֱלֹהֵנוּ מֶלֶךְ הָעוֹלָם
‎אֲשֶׁר קִדְּשָׁנוּ בְּמִצְוֹתָיו וְצִוָּנוּ...

Barukh Ata Adonay Eloheynu Melekh Ha'Olam,
asher kid'shanu b'mitzvotav v'tzivanu . . .

I. Lighting Shabbos candles:

(*Note:* While a *brakha* is usually recited just *before* one performs a *mitzvah*, the reverse is the case here: First light the candles, and then recite the *brakha* with your eyes closed or shielded from the candle light by your hands. Then open your eyes to see the light and fulfill the *mitzvah*.)

...לְהַדְלִיק נֵר שֶׁל שַׁבָּת.

... *l'hadlik ner shel Shabbat:* to kindle the lights of Shabbat.

2. **Lighting candles to begin Yom Kippur or a festival:**

...לְהַדְלִיק נֵר שֶׁל יוֹם טוֹב.

... *l'hadlik ner shel Yom Tov:* to kindle the lights of the festival.

...לְהַדְלִיק נֵר שֶׁל יוֹם הַכִּפּוּרִים.

... *l'hadlik ner shel Yom Ha'Kippurim:* to kindle the lights of Yom Kippur.

3. **Lighting Chanukah candles:**

...לְהַדְלִיק נֵר שֶׁל חֲנֻכָּה.

... *l'hadlik ner shel Chanukah:* to kindle the lights of Chanukah.

4. **Upon immersing in the waters of a *mikvah*:**

...עַל הַטְבִילָה.

... *al ha't'vilah:* concerning immersion.

5. **When washing hands** (dedicating one's hands to sacred purpose, upon arising and before a meal):

...עַל נְטִילַת יָדָיִם.

... *al n'tilat yadayim:* regarding the elevating of our hands.

6. **When affixing a *mezuzzah* to a doorpost:**

...לִקְבֹּעַ מְזוּזָה.

... *likboa mezuzzah:* to attach a *mezuzzah*.

7. **When putting on a *tallis*:**

...לְהִתְעַטֵּף בַּצִּיצִת.

... *l'hitateyf ba'tzitzit:* to wrap oneself in the fringes (of a tallis)

8. **When placing *t'fillin* on one's arm:**

...לְהָנִיחַ תְּפִלִּין.

... *l'haniach t'fillin:* to put on *t'fillin.*

and on one's head:

...עַל מִצְוַת תְּפִלִּין.

... *al mitzvat t'fillin:* concerning the *mitzvah* of *t'fillin.*

9. **When commencing a session of Torah study or Jewish spiritual teaching:**

...לַעֲסוֹק בְּדִבְרֵי תוֹרָה.

... *la'asok b'divrei Torah:* to engage in words of Torah.

10. **When sitting in the *sukkah* for a meal:**

...לֵישֵׁב בַּסֻּכָּה.

... *leysheyv ba'sukkah:* to sit/dwell in the *sukkah.*

11. **When ritually shaking the *lulav* (palm branch) and *etrog* (citron) during the fall festival of Sukkot:**

...עַל נְטִילַת לוּלָב.

... *al n'tilat lulav:* concerning the lifting up of the palm branch.

III. *Brakhot* Drawn from the Order of Jewish Daily Prayer

...בָּרוּךְ אַתָּה יהוה אֱלֹהֵינוּ מֶלֶךְ הָעוֹלָם

Barukh Ata Adonay Eloheynu Melekh Ha'Olam ...

1. **Awe for the wondrous complexity of our bodies:**

...אֲשֶׁר יָצַר אֶת הָאָדָם בְּחָכְמָה,

... *asher yatzar eht ha'adam b'chokhmah:* who fashioned human beings with wisdom;

2. Gratitude upon awakening in the morning to find one's soul and life restored anew.

This *brakha* concludes a song of praise for the purity and divine origin of the soul.

...הַמַּחֲזִיר נְשָׁמוֹת לִפְגָרִים מֵתִים.

... ha'machazir n'shamot lifgarim meytim: who returns souls to the perished.

3–17. These fifteen *brakhot* are central to the morning blessings. Each action involved in waking, rising, dressing, and embarking upon the day is an opportunity for a new *brakha*.

3. For consciousness itself:

נָתַן לַשֶּׂכְוִי בִינָה לְהַבְחִין בֵּין יוֹם וּבֵין לָיְלָה.
...אֲשֶׁר

... asher natan la'sekhvi vinah l'havchin beyn yom u'veyn lailah: who has given the mind the capacity to distinguish between day and night.

4. For being made in the divine image:

...שֶׁעָשַׂנִי בְּצַלְמוֹ.

... sheh' asani b'tzalmo: who made me in the divine image.

5. For being free:

...שֶׁעָשַׂנִי בֶּן/בַּת חוֹרִין.

... sheh'asani ben [men]/bat [women] chorin: who made me free.

6. For being Yisrael/of the people Israel/a God-wrestler:

...שֶׁעָשַׂנִי יִשְׂרָאֵל.

... sheh'asani Yisrael: who made me of the people Israel.

7. For opening our eyes to see:

‏...פּוֹקֵחַ עִוְרִים.

...pokeyach ivrim: who gives sight to the blind.

8. For donning a robe or undergarment:

‏...מַלְבִּישׁ עֲרֻמִּים.

...malbish arumim: who clothes the naked.

9. For sitting up and stretching:

‏...מַתִּיר אֲסוּרִים.

...matir asurim: who frees the captive.

10. For getting out of bed:

‏...זוֹקֵף כְּפוּפִים.

...zokeyf k'fufim: who straightens the bent.

11. For standing on the floor:

‏...רוֹקַע הָאָרֶץ עַל הַמָּיִם.

...roka ha'aretz al ha'mayim: who stretches out the earth upon the waters.

12. For walking forward to meet the day's challenges and opportunities:

‏...הַמֵּכִין מִצְעֲדֵי גָבֶר.

...ha'meykhin mitz'adey gaver: who makes firm a person's steps.

13. When putting on shoes, symbolic of the protection we need to go forward:

‏...שֶׁעָשָׂה לִי כָּל צָרְכִּי.

...sheh'asah li kol tzorki: who provides me with all I need.

14. For getting dressed:

‏...אוֹזֵר יִשְׂרָאֵל בִּגְבוּרָה.

...ozeyr Yisrael bi'g'vurah: who girds Israel with strength.

15. For our headcovering, crowning us with a reminder of the
    Divine Presence:

    ‏...עוֹטֵר יִשְׂרָאֵל בְּתִפְאָרָה.

    ... *oteyr Yisrael b'tifarah:* who crowns Israel with splendor.

16. For feeling the exhaustion of the night pass away and day-
    time strength return:

    ‏הַנּוֹתֵן לַיָּעֵף כֹּחַ.

    ... *ha'noteyn la'ya'eyf ko'ach:* who gives strength to the weary.

17. For waking fully to greet the day:

    ‏הַמַּעֲבִיר שֵׁנָה מֵעֵינָי וּתְנוּמָה מֵעַפְעַפָּי.

    ... *ha'ma 'avir sheynah mey'eynay u't'numah mey'afapay:* who removes
    sleep from my eyes and slumber from my eyelids

18–20 These three *brakhot* surround the *Shema,* the thrice-daily
affirmation of divine unity and infinity. Together they are known
as the *Shema* and her blessings. The *brakha* for divine light stresses
the exclamatory syllable "oh!"; the *brakha* for divine love, the more
gentle "ah." The *Shema* unites light and love in the epiphany of
God's Oneness. From the vantage point of that peak experience we
are bathed in the original light of Creation and feel the vast love of
divine guidance, Torah, and *mitzvot.* Enlightened and loved, we see
into the future and glimpse a redemptive vision of human perfection and the fulfillment of Creation's purpose.

18. In gratitude for the original act of Creation, light and
    dark, day and night, the canopy of stars, the rhythms of
    the seasons, and the renewal of each day.

At night:

...אֲשֶׁר בִּדְבָרוֹ מַעֲרִיב עֲרָבִים,

... asher bi'dvaro ma'ariv aravim: who blends the evening light;

daytime:

...יוֹצֵר אוֹר וּבוֹרֵא חֹשֶׁךְ, עֹשֶׂה שָׁלוֹם וּבוֹרֵא אֶת הַכֹּל.

... yotzeyr or u'vorey choshekh, oseh shalom u'vorey et ha'kol: who fashions light and creates darkness, who is the maker of peace and creator of all.

19. **In gratitude for God's love:**

בָּרוּךְ אַתָּה יהוה, אוֹהֵב עַמּוֹ יִשְׂרָאֵל.

Barukh Ata Adonay oheyv amo Yisrael: A Fountain of Blessings are You *Adonay,* who lovingly cherishes your people Israel.

20. **In gratitude for the moments in which seemingly insurmountable obstacles fall away and we can move onward toward new possibilities:**

ברוּךְ אַתָּה יהוה, גָּאַל יִשְׂרָאֵל.

Barukh Ata Adonay ga'al Yisrael: A Fountain of Blessings are You *Adonay,* saving power of Israel.

(*Brakhot* 18–20 are each part of longer versions which can be found in any Hebrew prayerbook.)

IV Crafting New *Brakhot*

Many contemporary Jews are experimenting with new formulations of traditional blessings, and also inventing new blessings for the many circumstances of life that the traditional blessings may not cover.

The structure of an innovative *brakha* should address God by any of the Divine Names, and invoke a quality of God that induces the Divine Flow *(Malkhut).*

To cast a *brakha* in feminine God-language, one might employ בְּרוּכָה אַתְּ יָהּ *Brukhah Aht Yah* instead of *Barukh Ata Adonay.* To avoid the gendered Hebrew "You," a *brakha* could be formed in a way that emphasizes the "we" who bless, by beginning נְבָרֵךְ אֶת *N'varekh et,* Let us bless . . . You may see *Shekhinah* invoked directly by using her name in lieu of *Eloheynu,* or perhaps a more gender-neutral phrase will be used, like עֵין הַחַיִּים *Eyn Ha'Chayyim,* describing God as the Source or Wellspring of Life. *Melekh Ha'Olam* sometimes cedes to *Chey Ha'Olamim,* Life-Force of All the Worlds, or *Ruach Ha'Olam,* Spirit, or Soul, of the World.

Thus one could craft the opening phrase of a Hebrew *brakha* to read:

בְּרוּכָה אַתְּ יָהּ שְׁכִינָה חֵי הָעוֹלָמִים...

Brukhah Aht Yah Shekhinah, Chey Ha'Olamim. . . .

A Fountain of Blessings are You *Shekhinah,* Life-Force of All the Worlds. . . .

or perhaps:

בָּרוּךְ אַתָּה יהוה עֵין הַחַיִּים רוּחַ הָעוֹלָם...

Barukh Ata Adonay Eyn Ha'Chayyim, Ruach Ha'Olam . . .

A Fountain of Blessings are You *Adonay,* Wellspring of Life, Soul of the World. . . .

or perhaps blending the more customary language with other names and attributes, as in:

בָּרוּךְ אַתָּה יהוה אֱלֹהֵינוּ חֵי הָעוֹלָמִים...

Barukh Ata Adonay Eloheynu, Chey Ha'Olamim . . .

The blessings in this appendix represent only a sampling of the variety of Hebrew *brakhot* which you may choose to draw upon. It is also entirely permissible to use one's own vernacular language in creating and offering a *brakha*. For example, Rabbi Rami Shapiro has interpretively rendered the Morning Blessings in this way:

בָּרוּךְ אַתָּה יהוה אֱלֹהֵנוּ מֶלֶךְ הָעוֹלָם...

Barukh Ata Adonay Eloheynu Melekh Ha'Olam...

Blessed is the Source of Life of all the World...

...whose Image is mirrored in my own.

...whose Freedom challenges me to be free.

...whose Teaching makes of me a Jew.

...whose Wisdom opens the blind eye.

...whose Compassion commands us to clothe the naked.

...whose Justice bids us to free the captive.

...whose Love calls us to lift the fallen.

...whose Unity demands that we care for all life.

...whose Being provides us with infinite possibilities.

...whose Torah guides my every step.

...whose Wonder removes sleep from my eyes, that I might awake to the wonder of Life!

You may wish to experiment with this model yourself, beginning a *brakha* in Hebrew and then offering any expression of gratitude or praise which the moment calls for. Naturally, a *brakha* recited entirely in English is also fine. Be creative!

I invite you to become a joyous explorer on the Path of Blessing.

Notes

❦

Introduction

A world that is shaking underfoot—Arthur Waskow, *Down-to-Earth Judaism: Food, Money, Sex and the Rest of Life* (New York: William Morrow, 1995), p. 6.

The Spiritual Practice of *Brakhot*

"When you feel a lack of understanding...."—Rav Abraham Isaac Kook, *Orot Ha'Kodesh* I:100, adapted from a translation by Ben Zion Bokser, *The Essential Writings of Abraham Isaac Kook* (New York: Amity House, 1988), p. 151.

"Live and take delight in all that is good...."—Rav Abraham Isaac Kook, *Orot Ha'Kodesh* I:84–5, from *The Classics of Western Spirituality: Abraham Isaac Kook*, translation and introduction by Ben Zion Bokser (Ramsey, NJ: Paulist Press, 1978), p. 209.

"Be holy!"—*kedoshim tih'yu*, Leviticus 19:1, and *vih'yitem kedoshim*, Leviticus 11:45.

B'khol d'rakhekha daeyhu—Proverbs 3:6.

Mochin d'gadlut / mochin d'katnut—Hasidic tradition, expanding upon kabbalistic sources, uses these terms to refer respectively to higher, more mature, or more ecstatic, and lower, more immature, or merely more mundane levels of consciousness. An excellent description of these states is found in the introduction to *Your Word Is Fire: The Hasidic Masters on Contemplative Prayer*, translated and edited by Arthur Green and Barry Holtz (Woodstock, VT: Jewish Lights, 1993).

This is the condition described as *galut*—Exile as a political condition is a painful separation from one's native land and one's proper place; as a spiritual condition, exile represents the concealment of the divine and our consequent anguished inability to experience God in our lives.

Just as every seventh day we separate out Shabbos—Shabbat (or Shabbos), the seventh day, is the final phase of Creation in which God ceases from creating the physical world and imparts consciousness to Creation. On Shabbat, by refraining from our own work in the material world, we can concentrate on personal and communal spiritual growth and thus pattern our days on a divine rhythm. The meaning and purpose of our six days of world-changing work is informed by the insights our Shabbat experience brings us.

Jews from an Eastern European (Ashkenazic) background frequently employ a pronunciation system that can render the letter *tav* as an "s" sound. Hence "Shabbat" becomes "Shabbos," *tallit* (prayer-shawl) becomes *tallis*, etc. (An even less frequent pronunciation influenced by Castilian Spanish uses a "th," hence "Sabbath"). In this work I employ "Shabbat" when quoting Torah or speaking formally. "Shabbos" evokes a warmer and more intimate feeling.

a *brakha* causes *shefa*, the "abundant flow"—Many commentaries on prayer and blessing explore the relationship between the rising up of yearning from "below" and the arousal of the divine flow from "above." Even Creation itself has been midrashically attributed to the arousal within God engendered by the contemplation of the good deeds of the righteous who were yet to be. The Talmudic commentator Rabbi Samuel Eliezer ben Judah HaLevi (1555–1631), known as the MaHaRSHa, an acronym for his Hebrew name, in his commentary on *Brakhot* 35b states: "*Brakhot* induce the *shefa*, the downward cycling of blessing from above."

In his great work *Shney Luchot Ha'Brit*, the Kabbalist and theologian Rabbi Isaiah Horowitz teaches: "There are two types of bestowal of *shefa*. The first is [continuous] for maintaining the world's existence, and the second depends on the deeds of those below." See *Isaiah Horowitz: The Generations of Adam*, translated by Miles Krassen (Mahweh, NJ: Paulist Press, 1996), p. 337. A related teaching attributed to the Baal Shem Tov appears in *Keter Shem Tov*, 194: "When a person eats a fruit or other food and recites a blessing over it with feeling, saying, 'Blessed are You, O God,' as soon as he mentions God's Name, that person ['s *brakha*] awakens the Life Force through which that fruit was created [and is sustained]. Cited in Rabbi Aryeh Kaplan, *The Light Beyond* (Brooklyn, NY: Maznaim Publishing, 1981), p. 108.

"Anyone who derives pleasure from this world without a *brakha* is stealing from God!"—Rabbi Chanina bar Popa, cited in the Babylonian Talmud, *Berakhot* 35b. Rabbi Chanina bar Popa was a Palestinian teacher who lived at the end of the third and beginning of the fourth century C.E. He was renowned in the field of *aggadah* and is cited in the Talmud and in many *midrashim*. The Babylonian Talmud is a monumental twelve-volume work which develops and expands upon an earlier collection of Jewish teaching, the Mishnah. (The word "Talmud" simply means "learning.") The Talmud is a vast repository of Jewish wisdom, interpretation, and commentary, of which the primary and most extensive Bablyonian version was compiled between ca. 200–500 C.E.

"Each of us," he says, "will be called to give account"—This text which elaborates on an earlier tradition from the Talmud (*Yerushalmi, Kiddushin 48b*) is from the *Pri Etz Hadar*—an eighteenth-century kabbalistic text on the festival of Tu b'Shevat, the "Festival of Trees," which falls on the 15th of the Hebrew month of Shevat. Called the "Rosh Ha'Shanah of trees" by second-century rabbis, under later kabbalistic influence the celebration became a time to reinvoke the flow of *shefa*, which flows like sap through the mystical tree of the *S'firot* (Divine Emanations). Translated by Rabbi Miles Krassen, unpublished manuscript.

"Your depression is connected to your insolence . . ."—from the poem "In Praise of Manners" by the thirteenth-century Islamic mystical poet Rumi, translated in *Night and Sleep* by Coleman Barks and Robert Bly (Cambridge, MA: Yellow Moon Press, 1981), unpaginated.

Why, then, would someone offer a blessing to God?—This query has been posed by rabbis and teachers over centuries because of the curious structure of a *brakha* which could make it appear that humans were "blessing" God. It would seem illogical that the realm of perfection and unity would require our blessings. Thus, for instance, we read in *Sefer Ha'Chinuch* 420, "It is for this reason [because God doesn't need our blessings] that *Barukh Ata* means not "You are blessed" but rather "You are the source of all blessings." See Rabbi Binyamin Forst, *The Laws of Brachos* (Brooklyn, NY: Mesorah Publications, 1991), p. 27.

On this subject, a legend is told in the Talmud of Rabbi Yishmael ben Elisha, who entered the Holy of Holies, the innermost room of the Temple, and heard God say to him, *"Barkheyni* (bless me)!" Rabbi Yishmael responded by asking God to allow the divine attribute of mercy to overtake that of strict justice. Because of Rabbi Yishmael's reply, *barkheyni* is interpreted to mean that God did not expect to be offered blessing, but wanted Yishmael to ask God to bestow divine blessings upon us. (Talmud, *B'rakhot* 7a).

"The essence of divinity is found in every single thing."—Rabbi Moshe Cordovero (1522–1570), also known as RaMaK, an acronym for his Hebrew name, was one of the great Kabbalists of sixteenth-century Safed. His work systemizes and expounds upon the entire range of kabbalistic thought until his time. This quote is from *Shi'ur Qomah* Modena Manuscript 206b, commenting on *Zohar* 3:141b *(Idra Rabba)*, translated by Daniel Matt in *The Essential Kabbalah* (HarperSanFrancisco, 1995), p. 24; and in *God and the Big Bang* (Woodstock, VT: Jewish Lights, 1996), p. 39. Cordovero continues: "There is nothing that is not pervaded by the power of divinity. . . . God is in everything that exists . . . present in everything, and everything comes into being from it. Nothing is devoid of divinity. Everything is within it; it is within everything and outside everything. There is nothing but it." Rabbi Moshe Cordovero, in *Elimah Rabbati* (Jerusalem: Achuzat Yisrael, 1966), 24d–25a, see Matt, *The Essential Kabbalah*, p. 24.

God is garbed in everything—Hasidic teachers, expounding on earlier kabbalistic themes, emphasized the importance of comprehending the God-saturated nature of all existence. From the Baal Shem Tov we learn: "God is present in every movement. Each movement and every word depends on divine power. This is the [true] meaning of the verse. 'The whole earth is filled with God's glory' (Isaiah 6:3). Even the physical world is one of God's garments. 'Glory' means garments." See *Sefer Baal Shem Tov, B'reshit* p. 15, and *Likkutim Yekarim* 17c. As did other hasidic teachers who followed, Rabbi Menachem Nachum of Chernobyl pursues this theme in his work *Sefer Meor Eynayim*, see ch. *Lekh Lekha* 10b.

A generation later, Rabbi Schneur Zalman of Liadi reemphasizes this teaching in his masterwork *Likkutey Amarim* known as the *Tanya*. Here he cites the Kabbalist Isaac Luria's earlier teaching on this subject, saying: "This same thought was expressed by the Ari (see p. 188), of blessed memory, when he said that even in [what would appear to be] completely inanimate matter, such as stones or earth or water, there is a soul and spiritual life-force. [Though seemingly inanimate, they are actually] the garbing or clothing of the letters spoken in the [initial] Ten [Divine] Utterances [of Creation] which give life and existence to inanimate matter." See *Tanya: Shaar Ha'Yichud V'Ha'Emunah*, ch. 1. Rabbi Schneur Zalman (1745–1812) was affectionately known to his Lubavitcher Hasidim as the Alter Rebbe (the Old Rabbi). He founded the Hasidic movement called ChaBaD, an acronym for *Chokhma, Bina* and *Da'at*, the first three of the ten *S'firot* (Divine Emanations). The *Tanya* was published in 1796 and is still widely studied today.

Menachem Nachum Twersky of Chernobyl (1730–1787), called the Chernobyler Rebbe, was a disciple first of the Baal Shem Tov and then of the Maggid of Mezrich. He founded the Twersky hasidic dynasty and made the Ukrainian town of Chernobyl a hasidic spiritual center in the late eighteenth century. His teachings, which reflect a mastery of

Kabbalah, are recorded in *Sefer* (literally "book," but denoting especially a work by a hasidic author) *Meor Eynayim* (Light of the Eyes), first published in 1797.

No place is empty of God—*Leyt atar panui mineh*—*Tikkuney Zohar, Tikkun* 57:91b; (see also *Berakhot* 10a; *Midrash Rabbah, B'Midbar* 12:4; *Shir Ha'Shirim Rabbah* 3:15; *Zohar* 3:257b, 3:225a.)

The Baal Shem Tov—Rabbi Israel ben Eliezer, known as the Baal Shem Tov (1698–1760), was the founder of Hasidism. A charismatic God-intoxicated personality, he traveled among the common people and stressed attachment to God through love and joyous devotional prayer rather than through the strict and less accessible discipline of Talmud study and conventional formal piety. A natural mystic, he reframed kabbalistic teaching and illuminated a path of personal and communal spiritual elevation. The everyday life experiences of each person, however humble, became ecstatic opportunities to embrace God's nearness. He attracted an expanding circle of followers who spread his and their own teachings throughout Eastern Europe.

"All the earth is filled with God's Glorious-Presence"—Isaiah 6:3.

Isaac Luria on holy sparks—Rabbi Isaac ben Solomon Luria (1534–1572), also known as *Ha'Ari*, "the [sacred] Lion," grew up in Egypt, where he began his mystical studies of the *Zohar* and earlier Kabbalists, and the work of the Kabbalist Moshe Cordovero, with whom he later studied in Safed. Lurianic Kabbalah includes his concepts of *tzimtzum* (God's vacating space in God's-Self in order to allow room for the Creation), *tikkun* (restoration of the outer and inner cosmos), and *moshiach* (the role of the Messiah in the redemptive process). Luria wrote only one work, a commentary on the *Zohar, Sifra D'Tzeni'uta (The Book of Concealment)*. Rabbi Chayyim Vital and other disciples collected and published his oral teachings after his death.

In the drama of creation described in Lurianic Kabbalah, sparks of divine light fell into physicality in the cataclysmic "shattering of the vessels" precipitated by the sheer force of the flow of divine energy through the universes that emanated from the *Ayn Sof*. These sparks of holy light are embedded throughout the material world, present in all matter. Thus, says the hasidic work *Noam Elimelekh*: "There is nothing in the world that does not contain a spark of holiness, giving it existence. If it did not have that spark, it would not exist!" (*Noam Elimelekh* by Rabbi Elimelekh of Lezensk, *Parashat Yitro* 41d.)

The eighteenth-century mystic Alexander Suskind, in his *Yesod V'Shoresh Ha'Avodah*, reminds us: "When you eat and drink, you experience enjoyment and pleasure from the food and drink. Arouse yourself every moment to ask in wonder, 'What is this enjoyment and pleasure? What is it that I am tasting?' Answer yourself, 'This is nothing but the holy sparks from the sublime, holy worlds that are within the food and drink.'" (Israel: 1968) 7:2, 60a.

Holy One of Blessing, may it come to pass.... This text is the invocation from *Pri Etz Hadar* translated by Rabbi Miles Krassen, unpublished manuscript.

Language and God

"Apprehend God in all things"—Meister Eckhart, from *Meditations with Meister Eckhart* by Matthew Fox (Santa Fe, NM: Bear & Company, 1993), p. 14.

... so too we can find that light within the Hebrew letters—The Baal Shem Tov teaches: "The 22 letters [of the Hebrew alphabet] are in our words of Torah and prayer. Every physical thing also contains these 22 letters, with which the world and everything in it were created.... These letters are clothed in physical worldly concepts, with many covers, garments, and shells. Inside these letters is the spiritual [power of God]." See *Sefer Baal Shem Tov, B'reishit* 11; *Toledot Yaakov Yosef, B'reishit* (8c); cited also in Rabbi Aryeh Kaplan, *The Light Beyond* (Brooklyn, NY: Maznaim Publishing, 1981), p. 81.

The Baal Shem Tov teaches further: "When you focus all your thought on the power of the words, you may begin to see the sparks of light that shine within them. The sacred letters are the chambers into which God pours God's flowing light. The lights within each letter, as they touch, ignite one another, and new lights are born." *Keter Shem Tov* 72b, cited in *Your Word Is Fire: The Hasidic Masters on Contemplative Prayer*, translated and edited by Arthur Green and Barry Holtz (Woodstock, VT: Jewish Lights, 1993), p. 46. See this entire work for exceptional selections from hasidic texts on this subject.

"Then God formed the human from the dusty earth"—Genesis 2:7.

The androgynous human in the Garden of Eden—In *Midrash Rabbah*, one of the great collections of midrashic teaching on Genesis, we read that Rabbi Yermiah ben Elazar taught: "When the Holy One, Blessed Be, created the original *Adam*, the Holy One created the *Adam* as an androgynous [bisexual] being, for it is written: 'Male and female created He them, and called their name *Adam*' (Genesis 5:1–2)." Rabbi Shmuel bar Nachman said: "When the Holy One created the *Adam*, God created the *Adam* double-faced, then God split the *Adam* and made the *Adam* of two backs, one on this side and one on the other side. To this it is objected, but it is written: "And God took *mi'tzalotav* [Gen. 2:21—usually translated "one of his ribs"]. *Mi'tzalotav* means one of his *sides*, replied he, as you read, And for the second side *(tzela)* of the tabernacle," etc. (Exodus 26:20). *Midrash Rabbah on B'reishit* (Genesis) 8:1.

name all other creatures—Genesis 2:19–20: "And יהוה *-Elohim* formed every beast of the field out of the *adamah*, earth, and every bird of the air; and brought them to the *Adam* to see what the *Adam* would call them; and whatever the *Adam* called every living creature, that was its name. And the *Adam* called out the names of all animals. . . ."

Each creature's "name" is its essence—The tradition that each created entity owes its existence to the permutation of spiritual energies or letters that constitute its name is of ancient origin. In the *Tanya*, Rabbi Schneur Zalman writes: ". . . life-force flows to the stone through combinations and substitutions of the letters . . . as is explained in the *Sefer Yetzirah* [a second-to-fifth-century Hebrew mystical text], until the combination of the name stone descends from the Ten [original] Utterances [of Creation] . . . and this is the life-force of the stone. And so it is with all created things in the world—their names in the Holy

Tongue are the very "letters of speech" which descend, degree by degree, by means of the Ten Utterances recorded in the Torah." *Sha'ar Ha'Yichud V'Ha'Emunah,* ch. I.

lashon kadosh—The power and divinity of language is a key theme in Jewish mystical tradition. Says scholar Gershom Scholem of the Kabbalists: "To them the holy tongue is not simply a means of expressing certain thoughts, born out of a certain convention and having a purely conventional character. . . . Hebrew . . . reflects the fundamental spiritual nature of the world." *Major Trends in Jewish Mysticism* (New York: Schocken Books, 1941), p 17. Says Rabbi Isaiah Horowitz: "The letters of the Torah are not [formed by] convention. They are rather *ruchaniyut* [spiritual energies], whose form is related to the inner aspect of their soul. . . . Moreover, even when they are in their existent state, that is, when they are written down, *ruchaniyut* rests on those letters. . . ." *Isaiah Horowitz: The Generations of Adam,* translated by Miles Krassen (Mahwah, NJ: Paulist Press, 1996), p. 150.

letters the atomic "building blocks"—*Sefer Yetzirah,* one of the earliest-known volumes of Jewish esoteric teaching, cryptically describes a complex process through which the Hebrew letters, as embodiments of divine intention, combine and recombine to produce the universe. This perception of Hebrew words and letters as the constituent spiritual elements of existence undergirds most Jewish mystical teaching. Says the Baal Shem Tov: "If these letters were removed even for an instant and returned to their Source . . . all the world (and) all created things would literally revert to absolute nothingness." Quoted by Rabbi Schneur Zalman in *Tanya, Sha'ar Ha'Yichud V'Ha'Emunah,* ch. I.

each Hebrew letter is also a number—*Gematria* is the practice of using the numerical values of Hebrew letters and words to add depth of meaning to the use of Hebrew language, and especially as an aid to the interpretation of Torah. For instance, "light" אור *or,* which is the first coming-into-existence at Creation, has the same numerical value, 207, as "mystery" רז *raz,* which can be taken to point us away from a literal and toward a more mysterious sense of the light which emanated from the Beyond before any sun existed.

"The old shall be made new and the new shall be made holy"—from the writings of Rav (Rabbi) Abraham Isaac Kook (*Iggerot Ha'Re'ayah* I, 164). Rav Kook (1865–1935) was a great twentieth-century Kabbalist, philosopher, and mystic. He served as chief rabbi of Palestine prior to the establishment of the State of Israel.

Barukh

"One glorious chain of love"—from "The Third Letter," in Rabbi Samson Raphael Hirsch, *The Nineteen Letters on Judaism* (New York: Philipp Feldheim Inc., 1960, translated by Rabbi Bernard Drachman and prepared by Jacob Breuer), p. 36.

"One should not toss a *brakha* from one's mouth"—Talmud, *Berakhot*, 47a.

Rashi adds: "A *brakha* should be said..."—from his commentary on Talmud *Berakhot* 47a. Rashi, an acronym for Rabbi Solomon ben Isaac (1040–1105), was a renowned commentator on the Bible and Talmud. He was born in Troyes, France, and his commentary blends literal and midrashic interpretations; Rashi's work was continued by his grandchildren, who founded the French school of Talmudic commentators called *Tosefot*.

kavvanah—The root *KVN* means "to clasp or fasten." Through *kavvanah* we attach our strength and focused intention to our words and actions. The Baal Shem Tov said: "Enter into every letter with all your strength. God dwells in each letter and as you enter it, you become one with God." (*Tzavaat Ha'Rivash* 13a)

Ayn Sof—The expression *Ayn Sof*—the "Without End" or "Without Limit"—has its origins in the work of early Kabbalists and the *Zohar,* where we read: "There is no end/limit to the light pouring out." (*Parashat Bo*) It is used to express the absolute and incomprehensible infinitude of the divine essence. In the *Etz Chayyim* (the classic kabbalistic text by Chayyim Vital which expounds upon Lurianic teachings) we read: "It is known that the upper light which continues higher and higher without end, which is called the *Ayn Sof*—the Endless, its name demonstrates that it is completely and essentially ungraspable. It is utterly abstract, apart from all thought, and prior to all things emanated, created, formed, and made. It has no time of origin or beginning, for it has always been and continues eternally." (*Etz Chayyim: Heykhal Adam Kadmon, Sha'ar Aleph* cited in Rabbi Shaul Baumann, *Sefer Miftechey Chochmat Ha'Emet,* ch.I: *Ayn Sof*).

God withdrew a point of God's pure essence...to create an opening—This teaching derives from the mystical teachings of the sixteenth-century Kabbalist Isaac Luria. "When in [the divine] simple will it was resolved to create worlds and emanate the emanations...[God] contracted [God's]self within the middle point of [God's]self, in the very center. And [God] contracted that Light, and it was withdrawn to the sides around the middle point. Then there remained an empty space, an atmosphere and a vacuum extending from the precise point of the center." From Chayyim Vital, *Etz Chayyim,* expounding Isaac Luria's teaching on *tzimtzum,* cited by Ben Zion Bokser in *The Jewish Mystical Tradition* (Ironstone, NJ, 1993), pp. 143–144; (See also *tzimtzum* p. 207)

emanations birthing time and space—Kabbalistic teaching, because of its sense of the Divine as a dynamic interplay of feminine and masculine qualities, boldly employs conception, pregnancy, and birthing imagery in descriptions of the process of creation. In particular, Kabbalah describes the descending emanations of Divinity which evolve the world as being born out of the "womb" of the *S'firah* (Divine Emanation) of *Binah*— often called "the Supernal Mother."

olam ha'pirud.... **This is the sphere of dimensionality and physicality in which we live**—The mystical tradition describes Creation as a chain of divine emanations which flow from the supernal realm of transcendent unity toward the multiplicity and dimensionality of the created world. *Olam ha'yichud* refers to the divine realm of unification beyond time or space; *olam ha'pirud (alma d'peruda* in the *Zohar*) is the world of separation, the domain that is the product of Creation.

"Yehi Or! **Let there be light!"**—Genesis I:3.

light as an already cooled energy—The creative process unfolds with successive degrees of concealment or cooling of the divine light, such that by the time the physical universe comes into existence, the light is maximally concealed.

teaches the Koznitzer Maggid—*Sefer Avodat Yisrael, Va'Yikra* 41. Rabbi Yisrael Hopstein, a founder of Polish Hasidism, was a disciple of the Maggid of Mezrich, Rabbi Levi Yitzhak of Berdichev, Rabbi Elimelekh of Lizhensk, and Rabbi Shmuel Shmelke of Nikolsburg. A great Talmudic scholar and master of kabbalistic tradition, he was also renowned as a passionate orator, teacher, healer, and miracle-worker. *Avodat Yisrael*, a commentary on the weekly Torah readings published in 1842, is among the most popular of his works.

222!—The sense that the sequence of root letters of *barukh* illustrates a progressive amplification is also captured in a teaching offered by Rabbi Binyomin Forst (elaborating on a teaching of Rabbi Yehuda Leove ben Betzalel, the sixteenth-century chief rabbi of Prague, who was known as the Maharal) on how the word *barukh* can carry the meaning of "increase." *Beyt* (2), following the unitive *alef* (1), indicates an increase in single digits, *khaf* (20), an increase in double digits, and *reysh* (200) an increase in triple digits. Thus a *brakha* can be understood as a supplication, urging God to let flow a multitude of blessings upon us. See Rabbi Binyomin Forst, *The Laws of Brachos* (Brooklyn, NY: Mesorah Publications, Ltd. 1990), pp. 28–29.

the One who, with goodness, makes "the beginning" anew each moment.—In the morning liturgy, part of the prayer text known as *Yotzeyr*, which praises God as the source of goodness, ever renewing creation.

Kol ha'neshama t'hallel Yah!... "Every soul breath praises God!"—From Psalm 150, recited in the morning liturgy.

Rabbi Avraham Ha'Malakh—This story is charmingly retold by Elie Wiesel: "Rabbi Avraham was a legend.... Sometimes he would say the first word of a prayer and lose himself in that word for hours. His powers of concentration were such that he wouldn't even feel the presence of those around him." *Sages and Dreamers* (New York: Touchstone, 1991), p. 392. Rabbi Avraham Ha'Malakh was the son of Rabbi Dov Baer, the

Maggid of Mezrich, and the learning partner of Rabbi Schneur Zalman
of Liady. He died in 1776 at the age of 35.

**Jewish tradition teaches that we should be able to say one hundred
brakhot a day**—A tradition attributed to Rabbi Meir, cited in the
Talmud, *Menachot* 43b, in which the similar sound of the Hebrew words
"hundred" and "what" leads to an innovative interpretation: "It was
taught: R. Meir used to say, 'One is obligated to say one hundred *(meyah)*
blessings daily, as it is written [in Torah, Deut. 10:12]: And now, Israel,
what *(mah)* does יהוה your God require of you?' [Rabbi Meir invites us
to read this as: And now, Israel, a hundred *(meyah)* does in your God
require of you!] On Shabbat and on festivals it is said that R. Chiyya son
of R. Avia endeavored to make up this number by the use of spices and
delicacies."

The mystical dimension of this requirement was explored by the
thirteenth-century Spanish Kabbalist Yosef Gikatilla, in his work *Sha'arei
Orah*. Here he explains that the hundred blessings unite all the levels of
soul within a person and collectively for the people Israel. The hundred
blessings promote the flow of divinity into the world and help us achieve
good and prosperous lives. *Sha'arei Orah, Sha'ar Rishon* (Hebrew edition:
Yosef ben Shlomo, Jerusalem: Bialik Institute, 1970), p. 60. (see:
"יהוה" ... this is my Name forever, p. 204).

"All of your people are toads"—lyrics from the musical play *The King and
I*, music by Richard Rodgers, book and lyrics by Oscar Hammerstein II,
based on the novel *Anna and the King of Siam* by Margaret Landon. Lyrics
and musical score printed by Williamson Music, Inc., New York City.

"God was in this place..."—Genesis 28:16. This is Rabbi Lawrence
Kushner's translation of the biblical verse, and title of his book *GOD Was
in this PLACE & I, i Did Not Know* (Woodstock, VT: Jewish Lights, 1991),
which is his presentation of seven different methods of Torah study on
this verse.

**"And the man, Moshe, was more *anav* than any other human on the
face of the earth."**—Numbers 12:3. This teaching is recorded in
Likkutim Yekarim (p. 1), a collection of the teachings of the Baal Shem Tov

and the Maggid of Mezrich compiled by Rabbi Yissachar Baer of
Zlatchov, published in Lemberg, 1792. The Maggid was the preeminent
disciple and successor of the Baal Shem Tov. He earned the title Maggid
because of his gifted oratory and brilliant interpretations (see p. 47). He
continued the work of his teacher and spread the hasidic message of
hope, faith, and joy in the service of God throughout Eastern Europe.

"Yaakov!... Yaakov!"—Genesis 46:2.

"Moshe!... Moshe!"—Exodus 3:4.

Rabbi Shlomo of Radomsk taught—Rabbi Shlomo of Radomsk
(1803–1866) was appointed rabbi of Radomsk, Poland, in 1834 and
accepted as a hasidic leader a decade later. This teaching can be found in
his most famous work, *Tiferet Shelomoh,* and in Lawrence Kushner and
Kerry Olitzky, *Sparks Beneath the Surface* (Northvale, NJ: Jason Aronson,
Inc., 1993), p. 34.

"Avadim hayyinu...We were slaves..."—The beginning of the Passover
narrative in the Haggadah. It directly follows, and is in response to, the
Four Questions.

"slaves of time, they are slaves of slaves"—Yehudah ben Shemuel
HaLevi (1075?–1141) was the foremost Hebrew poet of the medieval
Jewish community of Spain. His work can be read in Hebrew, with
English translation by Nina Salaman, in *Selected Poems of Jehudah Halevi*
(Philadelphia: Jewish Publication Society, 1924), based on the critical
edition edited by Rav Chaim Brody, Chief Rabbi of Prague.

"Ears saw and eyes heard."—Louis Ginsberg cites this *midrash* in Volume
III of his work *The Legends of the Jews* (Philadelphia: Jewish Publication
Society, 1911), p. 106, and refers us also to also 4 Ezra 5.37; Philo, *Moses,*
2 (3).97. Rabbi Arthur Green cites *Mekhilta Yitro ba'chodesh* 9 (235) in *Seek
My Face, Speak My Name: A Contemporary Jewish Theology* (Northvale, NJ: Jason
Aronson Inc., 1992), p. 235.

A story is told of Rabbi Yosef Yitzhak Schneerson of Lubavitch—
(1880–1950). The sixth Lubavitcher Rebbe, he was a passionate orga-

nizer of Torah education throughout Communist Russia. He was arrested many times for "counter-revolutionary activities" and once sentenced to death, sparking worldwide protests and pleas for clemency. His death sentence was commuted and he continued his work. Ultimately he escaped the Nazi murderers to arrive in New York and build the Brooklyn-based Chabad Lubavitch Hasidic movement.

Moshe . . . was privileged to know the divine Essence—Exodus 34:6.

"Finite person, you can't be God"—*Midrash, Sifre Deuteronomy* 49.

on the sixth "day" God declared creation to be "very good."—Genesis 1:31.

tikkun, **a healing and repairing of creation**—*Tikkun* is the concept of the restitution or restoration of harmony in the inner and outer cosmos. Through our actions, our *mitzvot,* we can restore and return to their Source the divine sparks which scattered during the cataclysms of Creation. Human actions have mystical significance because they are linked with the secret workings of Creation, and because they are integrated into a vast cosmological drama which is enacted in order to rectify the flaws in the world and to restore everything to its proper place. Says Rav Kook: "Whenever a person raises him[/her]self through good deeds, through a higher stirring of his[/her] yearning for godliness, wisdom, justice, beauty, and equity, [s/]he perfects the spiritual disposition of all existence." (*Orot Ha'Kodesh III,* p. 314)

Ata

"Du, Du, Du"—Song of Rabbi Levi Yitzhak of Berdichev, disciple of the Maggid of Mezritch, who led the Hasidic community of Berdichev in Poland during the late 1700s until his death in 1810. His teachings are preserved in his work *Kedushat Levi,* a hasidic commentary on the weekly Torah readings.

"From my flesh I see God"—Job 19:26.

Isaac Luria—(see p. 188)

This concealing of the infinite grants us our existence . . . and "the illusion of our separate identity" . . . and "catch an authentic glimpse of true Oneness"—From the chapter "Seeking God: Look First to Love," in Rabbi Arthur Green, *Seek My Face, Speak My Name: A Contemporary Jewish Theology* (Northvale, NJ: Jason Aronson Inc., 1992), p. 27: "According to the Hasidic masters, the greatest gift God gives us is *tzimtzum* (literally, the 'contraction' of God), which to them means the illusion of our separate identity. Only bit by bit and by means of careful training are we allowed to peer beyond that veil, and always in doses that will nourish rather than destroy us. The vehicle for this growth process is the projected screen image, the shadow-play on the wall of our cave of individuation called the personal God. It is only by going through the path of personhood, ever striving toward a greater intimacy with that 'other,' that we can prepare ourselves to catch an authentic glimpse of true oneness. Judaism is a tradition that loves the person, that embraces the human as God's unique image in the world. *A Jewish path to oneness can only be one that leads through human intimacy.*"

Rabbi Abraham Joshua Heschel taught—I heard this from Rabbi Dr. Arthur Green, who studied with Rabbi Heschel. See also Arthur Green, *Seek My Face, Speak My Name*, p. 28. Rabbi Abraham Joshua Heschel (1907–1972) was a scholar and religious philosopher descended from the Maggid of Mezrich, the Apter Rebbe, and Rabbi Levi Yitzhak of Berdichev. He was for many years professor of Jewish ethics and mysticism at the Jewish Theological Seminary, and a prolific author.

Martin Buber (1878–1965), philosopher and theologian, Zionist leader and thinker, wrote his work *I and Thou* in 1925 in Germany, where he lived until 1938, when he moved to Palestine. Buber's understanding of the I-Thou quality present in genuine human relationships led him to experience God as the Eternal Thou, and to describe our true relationship with God as an I-Thou relation. God, the Eternal Thou, cannot be grasped intellectually, but can be felt through our relationships with people, and also animals, nature, or even sometimes works of art.

Rabbi Arthur Green writes: "Traditionally, every day in the life of a pious Jew is filled with the recitation of blessings. Each of these is ideally an opening to the heart to the 'Eternal Thou,' a reaching forth to embrace the transcendent in the intimacy of familiar form." Arthur Green, "Rethinking Theology," in *The Reconstructionist* (September 1988), pp. 8–13.

Buber's account of this story can be found in "Autobiographical Fragments" in *The Philosophy of Martin Buber*, Schilpp & Friedman, eds. (Library of Living Philosophers, Vol. XII, Open Court Publ. IL. 1967), pp. 25–26.

"all real living is meeting."—Martin Buber, *I and Thou* (New York: Charles Scribner's Sons, 1958), p. 11.

"All of Creation took place..."—*Zohar Raya Mehemna* 2:42b. The Chernobyler cites this teaching in *Meor Eynayim, Parashat Mikketz*, The Koznitzer Maggid in *Avodat Yisrael, Va'Yikra* 41a, and Rabbi Eliyahu DiVadish in the Introduction to *Reishit Chokhmah*, p. 2a.

prayer of the *kohanim*—called *Birkat Kohanim*, this ancient blessing is found in Numbers 6:24–26.

"the kiss"—*Zohar* 2:146a–b; see also Tishby, *Wisdom of The Zohar*, p. 364: "Another interpretation: 'Let him kiss me with the kisses of his mouth' (Song of Songs 1:2) What did King Solomon mean by introducing words of love between the upper and the lower world, and by beginning the praise of love, which he has introduced between them, with 'let him kiss me'? They have already given an explanation for this, and it is that inseparable love of spirit for spirit can be [expressed] only by a kiss, and a kiss is with the mouth, for that is the source and outlet of the spirit. And when they kiss one another, the spirits cling to one another, and they are one, and then love is one."

Moshe is said to have known God *"panim el panim*, face to face"— Deuteronomy 34:10.

"I am my beloved's and my beloved is mine."—Song of Songs 6:3.

In antiquity, the feminine form of "you" . . . —see, for example: Judges 17:2; II Kings 4:16; 4:23; 8:1; Jeremiah 4:30; Ezekiel 36:13.

"Any place where the masculine and the feminine are not both present, God is not fully present"—*Zohar, B'reishit* 55b: " 'Male and female [God] created them.' From this we learn that any image that does not embrace male and female is not a high and true image. The Blessed Holy One is not present (does not reside) in any place where the masculine and the feminine are not found together. See also many other references throughout *Zohar, B'reishit,* and also *Zohar, Va'Yikra* 7b.

Rabbi Arthur Green adds: "As the dualities of God and world, of *sovev* [surrounding] and *memaley* [filling], are meant to be overcome so too is the duality of male and female. It is a united male-female consciousness that reaches forth to *Ayn Sof.* This union takes place within the individual psyche as well as in the community of men and women. . . . within each person as well as . . . the species as a whole." *Seek My Face, Speak My Name,* p. 42.

"You are," says the *Tikkuney Zohar,* "the unity of all Your Names."— from *Patach Eliyahu,* a passage in the introduction to the *Tikkuney Zohar,* a commentary to the *Zohar* written around the year 1300. This passage was introduced into the Sephardic liturgy by Isaac Luria in the sixteenth century as a prelude to prayer.

"*Yah,* where shall I find You?"—poem by Yehudah HaLevi, in *Selected Poems of Jehudah Halevi* (Philadelphia: Jewish Publication Society, 1924), p. 134.

Naming God

"For the mind in harmony with the Tao"—Chinese Zen Master Seng-Ts'an (?–606), cited in Stephen Mitchell, *The Enlightened Heart* (New York: HarperCollins, 1989), p. 27.

"And when they ask me, 'What is His Name?' "—Exodus 3:13.

The Holy One "speaks" Creation into being—Genesis 1:3. The mystical tradition has never understood divine speech as literally comparable to human speech. The *Zohar*, for instance, describes God's utterance as a mystical birthing of energy from within the supernal realms: "This phrase *'va'yomer*, and [God] said,' opens the door to questioning and understanding. We define this 'saying' as an energy drawn from the secret limitlessness through the mystic power of *machshavah*, thought. 'And God said' means that the supernal palace [known as *Elohim*] generated from the holy seed with which it was pregnant... [and] bore in silence, without making a sound." *Zohar, B'reishit* 16b.

What is God's Name?—Text by the twelfth-century Christian mystic Meister Eckhart in *Meditations with Meister Eckhart*, introduction and versions by Matthew Fox (Santa Fe, NM: Bear & Co. 1983), p. 74.

"Leyt machshavah t'fisah bakh klal."—*Tikkuney Zohar* 17a, from *Patach Eliyahu*, a mystical text, included in many prayerbooks. The essence of God is beyond definition. Says Rav (Rabbi) Abraham Isaac Kook: "The essence of faith is an awareness of the vastness of infinity. Whatever conception of it enters the mind is an absolute negligible speck in comparison... to what really is. All [our descriptions merely] convey the yearning of the soul's original nature for what lies beyond everything. All the divine names, whether in Hebrew or in any other language, provide merely a tiny, dim spark of the hidden light for which the soul yearns when it says 'God.' Every definition of God leads to heresy; definition is spiritual idolatry." From Abraham Isaac Kook, *Orot.*

A noble thinker once challenged Buber—from "Autobiographical Fragments" in *The Philosophy of Martin Buber*, Schilpp & Friedman, eds. (Library of Living Philosophers, Vol. XII, Open Court Publ. IL. 1967), pp. 29–31.

"and they ask me, 'What is His name?' what shall I say to them?"—Exodus 3:13.

"Ehyeh Asher Ehyeh"—Exodus 3:14. Says the *Zohar:* R. Eleazar then asked his father to explain to him the name *Ehyeh Asher Ehyeh*. He said, "This name is all-comprehensive." *Zohar, Va'Yikra* 3:65a–b.

Before there was a before—Rabbi Arthur Waskow crafted this phrase to express the paradox of using temporal language to refer to a nontemporal dimension.

The Name Beyond Name

"Now the moment I flowed out from the Creator"—Text by Meister Eckhart in *Meditations with Meister Eckhart,* introduction and versions by Matthew Fox (Santa Fe, NM: Bear & Co. 1983), p. 12.

Every time we breathe, we breathe the Name of God—Rabbi Arthur Waskow has incorporated this teaching into much of his work. His liturgical poem *Nishmat,* published in 1989 as part of the P'nai Or Religious Fellowship *Siddur, Or Chadash,* excerpted here, expresses the wonder of our communion with God through breath:

> You whose very Name—
> YyyyHhhhWwwwHhhh—
> Is the Breath of Life,
> The breathing of all life
> Gives joy and blessing to your Name. . . .

> You are the breathing that gives life to all the worlds. . . .

> As we breathe out what the trees breathe in,
> And the trees breathe out what we breathe in,
> So we breathe each other into life,
> We and You.
> YyyyHhhhWwwwHhhh.

God breathed into the lifeless *Adam*-earthling's nostrils the breath-of-life, and the human became a living soul—See Genesis 2:7.

ripples of Creation energy still flow—For a magnificent account of the unfolding of the universe from the "primordial flaring forth" through the unfolding of human civilizations, see Brian Swimme and Thomas Berry, *The Universe Story* (San Francisco: HarperSanFrancisco, 1992).

Aleph

"I have put duality away"—Rumi, cited in *The Mystic Vision*, compiled by Andrew Harvey and Anne Baring (San Francisco: HarperSanFrancisco, 1995), p. 179.

"Says Isaiah: 'Peace to the one...'"—Rabbi Levi Yitzhak of Berdichev, *Sefer Kedushat Levi, Mishpatim*, p. 139, citing Isaiah 57:19.

the *Shema*—This affirmation of the all-inclusive unity and infinity of God has its source in Torah (Deuteronomy 6:4) and is central to the act of Jewish prayer. Yet, says Rabbi Arthur Green of the *Shema*, "the core of our worship is not a prayer at all, but a cry to our fellow-Jews and fellow-humans. In it we declare that God is one—which is also to say that humanity is one, that life is one, that joys and sufferings are all one—for God is the force that binds them all together." From the Prayerbook of the Reconstructionist Movement, *Kol Haneshamah, Shabbat Vehagim* (Wyncote, PA: Reconstructionist Press, 1994), p. 276.

Shekhinah—The term *Shekhinah* is an expansion of the biblical concept of *Kavod Ha'Shem*, the manifest presence of God. In post-Biblical literature *Shekhinah*, which derives from the root שכן ShKhN, to dwell, came to mean the feminine, in-dwelling experience of God. Jewish mystical literature elaborated this image of *Shekhinah* as the divine feminine. Jewish mystics thus have seen the unity of the divine realm as dependent upon the healing union of God's transcendent (masculine) and immanent (feminine) aspects, and have taught that the people Israel can promote this healing through prayer and Torah.

"Just as the Holy One condensed and concentrated the *Shekhinah*"— Rabbi Menachem Nachum of Chernobyl, *Sefer Meor Eyneyim, B'reishit*, p. 8.

"The Holy One Blessed Be He refers..."—From the teachings of the Baal Shem Tov, *Keter Shem Tov*, 401.

"Pick someone else."—Exodus 3:11, 13; 4:1, 10, 13. At the Burning Bush, Moshe hears God assigning him to return to Egypt and lead the people out of slavery. Reluctant to be chosen, Moshe responds with a list of objections.

Adonay

"When Barukh..."—This story is told of Rabbi Barukh of Mezbizh (1753–1811), grandson of the Baal Shem Tov. Martin Buber recounts it in his anthology *Tales of the Hasidim: The Early Masters* (New York: Schocken, 1947), p. 88. I have taken the liberty of returning the appellation "Divine Presence" to *Shekhinah*, assuredly the original Hebrew form.

"יהוה ... this is My Name forever"—This daring exegesis of Exodus 3:15 illustrates the capacity of a brilliant Kabbalist to see beneath the surface of a seemingly simple biblical phrase, and illuminate a mystical dimension. The Talmudic sages (*Pesachim 50a*) had observed that the Hebrew text of this phrase uses the word *l'olam* (usually translated "forever") in an unusual spelling, called *chaseyr*, or "deficient," because of the absence of the vowel-holding *waw (vav)*. While an allowable spelling for *l'olam*, it accentuates the root letters and suggests an equally appropriate translation: "hidden." Gikatilla follows Rashi's commentary on this passage, bypassing the more literal translation: יהוה ... this is my name forever, in favor of: יהוה ... this is my hidden (unpronounceable) Name!" *"Zeh zichri*, this is my memorial ..." he understands alternatively as a direct reference to *Adonay*, the name that refers to the immanent Divine Presence, the *S'firah* of *Malkhut* and the *Shekhinah*. It is this immanent Name, *Adonay*, near to us and not hidden, that is employed in place of the transcendent, concealed name in spoken prayer and blessing. Yosef Gikatilla, *Sha'arey Orah, Sha'ar Rishon* (Hebrew edition: Yosef ben Shlomo, Jerusalem: Bialik Institute, 1970), p. 79.

Yosef Gikatilla wrote *Sha'arey Orah* in thirteenth-century Spain, as a compendium of Jewish mystical teaching on the divine names in order to assist seekers in their quest for intimacy with God. The work was recently translated by Avi Weinstein and published by HarperCollins as *Gates of Light: Sha'are Orah* (1994).

Brikh Rachamana—Talmud, *Berakhot* 42.

In Jewish (as in Islamic) tradition we call the One by many descriptive Names—Yosef Gikatilla says: "Try with all [your] strength to comprehend the meaning of each of the Holy Names [of God] as they are recorded in Torah.... Then when [you] know the purpose of every Name [you] will realize the greatness of 'The One who spoke and the world came into being....' The Four-Letter-Name ... is like the trunk of a tree ... and the rest of the Holy Names are like branches, each with a different fruit.... All the words of Torah are woven into the tapestry of God's Names"—From the introduction to *Sha'arey Orah*, pp. 47–48.

In a classical text of the Islamic mystical tradition, we read: " 'Call on Allah [God], or call on the Beneficent. By whatever [name] you call on Him, He has the most beautiful names *(Sura Bani Isra'il. 110).'* Our master the Prophet says, 'Allah Most High has ninety-nine Names. Whoever learns them enters Paradise....' The Name which belongs to the Essence is only one; it is reflected as a thousand attributes in those who receive it." 'Abd al-Qadir al-Jilani (1077–1166), *The Secret of Secrets,* interpreted in English by Shaykh Tosun Bayrak al-Jerrahi (Cambridge, Eng.: Islamic Texts Society, 1992), p. 21.

the Place—The word *makom,* "place," has long been understood as actually being a divine Name. The teaching implicit in this name is that God is the address of the cosmos, the ultimate "place" within which the Creation resides. God is the overarching context of all existence. Concerning this we read in *Midrash Rabbah, B'reishit* 68:9: "[God] is the Place of the world; not the world God's place."

"There are so many gates in the House of the One"—Yosef Gikatilla, *Sha'arey Orah, Sha'ar Rishon* (Hebrew edition. Yosef ben Shlomo, Jerusalem: Bialik Institute, 1970), pp. 53/55.

"From the Name יהוה all the channels flow and are drawn to *Adonay...*"—Yosef Gikatilla, *Sha'arey Orah, Sha'ar Rishon* (Hebrew edition. Yosef ben Shlomo, Jerusalem: Bialik Institute, 1970), p. 57.

The [God within the] human self is called by the name *Adonay*— Rabbi Menachem Nachum of Chernobyl, *Sefer Han'hagot Yesharot.*

"The Presence of the Creator fills the earth. No place is empty!"— Rabbi Menachem Nachum of Chernobyl, *Sefer Meor Eyneyim, Parashat Lekh Lekha,* p. 20, citing *Tikkuney Zohar* 57:91b.

She is the gate of which the Zohar speaks—*Zohar* 1:7b.

adanim—Exodus 36:26. (This observation concerning *Adonay* and *adanim* is also noted by Yosef Gikatilla, ibid., p. 60.)

"Since the whole world is garbed in God," he said—*Sefer Meor Eyneyim, Parashat B'reishit.*

Shir Ha'Kavod, the mystical "Hymn of Glory"—written by the philosopher-poet Judah the Pious (d. 1217), it is included as a supplemental hymn in the order of prayer. For an accessible version with translation by Israel Zangwill, see p. 58, *Sabbath and Festival Prayerbook*, Morris Silverman, ed. (Rabbinical Assembly of America, 1946).

Eloheynu

"It is therefore written…"—*Sefer Baal Shem Tov, Va'Yelekh* 7; *Sefer Toldot Yaakov Yosef, B'reishit* 7, quoting in Deut. 31:18. See also *Keter Shem Tov* 85; "When a person realizes that God is hidden, God is really not so hidden at all! The [evil/perceptual] barriers crumble… and nothing can separate that person from God."

"I am closer to you than yourself…" Ibn Al Arabi, cited in *The Mystic Vision*, compiled by Andrew Harvey and Anne Baring (San Francisco: HarperSanFrancisco, 1995), p. 51.

Eloheynu/Elohim—*Elohim* is the most basic Hebrew term for God. (*Eloheynu* is possessive—"our God," the God close to, and experienced by, us.) It is a plural form of the singular *Eloha*, which is used only very rarely. But while plural in form, *Elohim* is singular in meaning and is characteristically used with singular verb forms and pronouns, calling dramatic attention to the overarching unity of all our diverse experiences of divinity.

I am יהוה your *Elohim* / *Anokhi* יהוה *Elohekha*—Numbers 15:4.

In his famous work… Rabbi Schneur Zalman of Liadi—*Sha'ar Ha'Yichud v'Ha'Emunah*, ch. 4.

praising יהוה as *Ha'Gadol* and *Ha'Gibor*—Deuteronomy 10:17. These references from Deuteronomy are understood by this great teacher as explicit kabbalistic references to the *S'firot* (Divine Emanations) of *Chesed* and *Gevurah*.

tzimtzum—A paradoxical term used both for the withdrawal (and consequent concealment) of God into God's Self in order to create space for Creation, a concept developed by Rabbi Isaac Luria, and for the radical condensing of God within Creation such that God's Presence and Oneness can be revealed.

"There is no place empty of God"—*Tikkuney Zohar* 57:91b.

As the medieval master Kabbalist Moshe Cordovero proclaimed— From the *Shi'ur Qomah Modena Manuscript* 206b cited in Matt, *The Essential Kabbalah*, p. 24.

"When a person realizes that God is hidden..."—*Sefer Baal Shem Tov, Va'Yelekh* 7; *Sefer Toldot Yaakov Yosef, B'reishit* 7; see also *Keter Shem Tov* 85.

surrounding and filling: *sovev* and *memaley*—These kabbalistic terms refer to our experience of God as both transcendent and immanent: utterly beyond and intrinsically within our world. As with all apparent dualisms, this sense of contrasting divine natures too is meant to be overcome.

"יהוה *Elohim* is a sun and a shield"—Psalm 84:12.

The lesson of *Elohim*—The Maggid of Mezrich teaches in the name of the Baal Shem Tov that God gives divine abundance in two ways— through love and through constriction. Love causes the divine abundance to flow. Through constriction the abundance is modulated so that it can descend from the higher realm of unity into the lower world of distinctions. Thus even constriction was originally an act of love. See *Maggid Devarav l'Yaakov* 102.

Aleynu—Since the fourteenth century this affirmation of the Oneness of God, and our hope for the perfection of the world, closes all congregational worship on weekdays, *Shabbat*, and festivals.

Melekh

"Through 'kingship' . . ."—Attributed to the Baal Shem Tov (quoting Job 19:26) by his disciple Rabbi Yaakov Yosef of Polnoye, in *Sefer Toledot Yaakov Yosef, Parashat Lekh Lekha,* 19a.

"Oh wonders of wonders!" Meister Eckhart, Tractate II, cited in *The Mystic Vision,* compiled by Andrew Harvey and Anne Baring (San Francisco: HarperSanFrancisco, 1995), p. 187.

"No more Big Daddy"—Rabbi Shefa Gold, song lyrics published in P'nai Or Religious Fellowship *Siddur, Or Chadash,* p. s-2, recorded in her self-produced 1987 album "Shema: Songs of Renewal and Jubilation."

Like *Adonay, Malkhut* . . . also became associated with *Shekhinah* . . . —see, for instance, Scholem, *Major Trends in Jewish Mysticism* (New York: Schocken Books, 1941): ". . . [a] fountain which springs from the heart of the mystical Nothing . . . flows through all the *Sefiroth* and through all hidden reality, until at last it falls into the 'great sea' of . . . *Malkhut,* the 'kingdom' of God, usually described in the Zohar as . . . the *Shekhinah.*" (pp. 220, 213)

"Even more than the calf wants to nurse, the cow wants to give suck"—Talmud, *Pesahim* 112a.

we can become the "throne"—The midrashic literature (see *B'reishit Rabbah* 47:8, 82:7) and the *Zohar* (see 1:213b, 3:182a, 3:217a, 3:262b) call the patriarch Yaakov a "throne" for the Divine Presence. It is understood that he had become such a holy vessel that he could receive the Glory of God. The Koznitzer Maggid (citing Cordovero's *Tomer Devorah*) reminds us that we can each become a throne by emulating the ten qualities of holiness that correspond to the ten *S'firot* (Divine Emanations). *Sefer Avodat Yisrael, B'reishit* I.

Ha'Olam

"The Name יהוה is beyond all Time"—Rabbi Schneur Zalman of Liadi, *Tanya: Sha'ar Ha'Yichud V'Ha'Emunah,* ch. 7.

"A blinding spark flashed"—*Zohar* 1:15a.

"With the appearance of the light, the universe expanded"—Kabbalist Shimon Lavi, *Ketem Paz* 1:124c, cited by Matt in *The Essential Kabbalah* (San Francisco: HarperSanFrancisco, 1995), p. 91.

Einstein said: Albert Einstein and Leopold Infeld, *The Evolution of Physics* (New York: Simon and Schuster, 1938), p. 31, cited by Gary Zukav in *The Dancing Wu Li Masters: An Overview of the New Physics* (New York: William Morrow, 1979), p. 35.

"If we imagine the North American continent to represent our galaxy"—Peter Russell, *The Global Brain* (New York: J. P. Tarcher, 1983), pp. 234–236.

"One of the most surprising and puzzling features of the universe"—Rupert Sheldrake, *The Rebirth of Nature* (Rochester, VT: Park Street Press, 1994), pp. 94–95.

"The smallest object that we can see"—Gary Zukav, *The Dancing Wu Li Masters: An Overview of the New Physics* (New York: William Morrow, 1979), p. 57.

"...the fundamental process of Nature lies outside space-time but generates events that can be located in space-time"—Physicist Henry Stapp, in *Nuovo Cimento* 40B 191–199, cited by Dr. Amit Goswami, *The Self-Aware Universe: How Consciousness Creates the Physical World* (New York: J. P. Tarcher, 1993), p. 61.

"inter-are"—This term was introduced by the Vietnamese Buddhist teacher Thich Nhat Hanh.

As the Baal Shem Tov said . . . —Stressing yet again the God-saturated nature of existence. *Likkutim Yekarim; Sefer Baal Shem Tov, V'Etchanan; Tzavaat Ha'Rivash* 233–234.

As Rav Kook proclaimed, "We cannot identify the abundant vitality within all living beings . . ."—*Orot Ha'Kodesh* 2:374, cited in Matt, *The Essential Kabbalah* (HarperSanFrancisco, 1995), p. 153.

"The ultimate meaning and purpose of life . . . cannot properly be thought."—Bede Griffiths, *Return to the Centre* (HarperCollins Ltd.

London, 1976), cited in *Mystic Vision*, compiled by Andrew Harvey and Anne Baring (HarperSanFrancisco, 1995), p. 15.

"O how may I ever express that secret word?"—from the collected oral recitations of sixteenth-century Indian mystic poet Kabir, from *One Hundred Poems of Kabir* (London: Macmillan & Co., 1961) cited in *The Mystic Vision*, compiled by Andrew Harvey and Anne Baring (HarperSanFrancisco, 1995), p. 50.

"God created all things in such a way that they are not outside of God's self"—from *Meditations with Meister Eckhart*, introduction and versions by Matthew Fox (Santa Fe, NM: Bear & Co., 1983), pp. 22–23.

"*Adonay*, You are the dwelling place!"—Psalm 90:1 Also see *B'reishit Rabbah:* The Holy One of Blessing is the Place of the *Olam*, not the *Olam* God's place. Rabbi Isaac said: It is evident that the Holy One is the dwelling place of the universe, and not the universe God's dwelling place. See note, "the Place," p. 205.

"In the beginning, there was existence alone"—From the Chandogya Upanishad in *The Upanishads*, translated by Swami Prabhavananda and F. Manchester (New York: Mentor Books, 1957), cited in Matt, p. 154.

Concluding a *Brakha*

"Then you gather everything...."—Rav Abraham Isaac Kook, *Orot Ha'Kodesh* 3:270; translated by D. Matt in *The Essential Kabbalah* (HarperSanFrancisco 1995) p. 124.

Isaac Luria reminds us: "By saying a *brakha* before you enjoy something, your soul partakes spiritually...."—See *Likkutey D'Torah* by Chayyim Vital, *Parashat Ekev.* This text is translated by D. Matt in *The Essential Kabbalah*, p. 149, citing a Lurianic *"Kavvanah* on Eating" recorded by Joseph Don Don, ca. 1570. See his footnote, p. 214.

Says the Maggid: "Place all your thoughts into the power of your words...."—*Maggid D'varav L'Yaakov (Likkutey Amarim)* 52.

Using a *Brakha* to Introduce a *Mitzvah*

"Fix your mind on Me"—*The Bhagavad Gita,* Text 65 of the final chapter (transl. Juan Mascaro, Penguin Classics, London, 1962). The *Bhagavad Gita* is the classic text of India's Vedic spiritual wisdom.

"There is no greater path than this. For wherever you go and whatever you do—even mundane activities—you serve God"—Rabbi Levi Yitzhak of Berdichev in *Sefer Kedushat Levi, Parashat Va'Yeshev,* 26a–b, cited in D. Matt, *The Essential Kabbalah* (HarperSanFrancisco, 1995), p. 151.

"domesticating the peak experience"—A phrase I heard from my teacher Rabbi Zalman Schachter-Shalomi.

walks facing God—Genesis 6:9 and 17:2.

The covenants undertaken by Noah and Avraham—Genesis 9:11 and Genesis 17:2–27 respectively.

"stand again at Sinai"—This phrase has become well known as the title of a groundbreaking work by Judith Plaskow, *Standing Again at Sinai: Judaism from a Feminist Perspective* (HarperSanFrancisco, 1990), which explores the implications of feminism for the transformation of Jewish life.

heard with their eyes and saw with their ears—(see p. 196).

God answered him *"b'kol"*—Exodus 19:19.

Moshe, they say, heard God speak . . . as his own voice"—*Midrash Rabbah, B'Midbar* 14:3; also cited in *Midrash Tehillim* 18:29 and 24:11.

"unripe fruit of divine wisdom"—*B'reishit Rabbah* 17:5: Torah is an unripe fruit of supernal wisdom. Daniel Matt called my attention to this teaching, which he has cited in *The Essential Kabbalah* (HarperSanFrancisco, 1995), pp. 145, 213.

The Kotzker Rebbe . . . "Where is God?"—*Emet V'Emunah,* p. 97. Rabbi Menachem Mendel Morgenstern of Kotzk (1787–1859), popularly known as the Kotzker Rebbe, was the disciple of the Seer of Lublin and Rabbi Simcha Bunim of Pshis'cha. He preached fierce loyalty to the truth and a stripping away of falsehood, deception, and hypocrisy as a path to God. His teachings are recorded in *Emet V'Emunah*, first published in Jerusalem in 1940.

"Where are you?"—Genesis 3:9.

"If your works are to live..."—Meister Eckhart, from *Meditations with Meister Eckhart* by Matthew Fox (Santa Fe, NM: Bear & Co., 1993), p. 98.

"To be in alignment with you"—Psalm 40:9.

"Every vision born of Earth is fleeting"—Rumi, cited in *The Mystic Vision*, compiled by Andrew Harvey and Anne Baring (HarperSan-Francisco, 1995), p. 112.

"If the only prayer..."—Meister Eckhart, from *Meditations with Meister Eckhart* by Matthew Fox (Santa Fe, NM: Bear & Company, 1993), p. 34.

A Note About the Author

ⲟ⳦ⳅⲟ

Rabbi Marcia Prager is a Reconstructionist/Jewish Renewal teacher, storyteller, artist, and therapist living and working in the Mt. Airy community of Philadelphia. A graduate of the Reconstructionist Rabbinical College, she also holds the personal *smicha* (rabbinic ordination) of Rabbi Zalman Schachter-Shalomi, the visionary leader of the Jewish Renewal Movement, with whom she has continued to work closely.

Marcia Prager serves as rabbi-*chaver* of the Philadelphia P'nai Or Religious Fellowship, the innovative Jewish community founded by Rabbi Schachter-Shalomi in 1973, and is the founding rabbi of a sister congregation, P'nai Or of Princeton, New Jersey. She has been appointed a pathfinder of the ALEPH Alliance for Jewish Renewal, a national organization which advances vital Judaism as an ethical and spiritual path, and serves ALEPH as director of professional development, designing programs of study leading to rabbinic ordination. She is on the faculty of the Jewish Renewal Life Center, a progressive Jewish learning program in Philadelphia, and teaches widely in many different Jewish and interfaith settings, offering the wisdom of Jewish tradition as a path of personal growth and world healing.

Rabbi Prager has also studied cultural anthropology, has an MFA in photography and drawing from Pratt Institute, New York, and taught for five years at the International Center of Photography in New York City.

She and her husband, *Hazzan* Jack Kessler, a traditionally trained cantor and director of two Jewish music ensembles, often lead retreats and workshops together.

OTHER BELL TOWER BOOKS

Books that nourish the soul, illuminate the mind,
and speak directly to the heart

Valeria Alfeyeva
PILGRIMAGE TO DZHVARI
A Woman's Journey of Spiritual Awakening
An unforgettable introduction to the riches of
the Eastern Orthodox mystical tradition. A modern *Way of a Pilgrim*.
0-517-88389-9 Softcover

Madeline Bruser
THE ART OF PRACTICING
Making Music from the Heart
A classic work on how to practice music which combines
meditative principles with information on body mechanics
and medicine.
0-517-70822-1 Hardcover

Melody Ermachild Chavis
ALTARS IN THE STREET
A Courageous Memoir of Community and Spiritual Awakening
A deeply moving account that captures
the essence of human struggles and resourcefulness.
0-609-80196-1 Softcover

Tracy Cochran and Jeff Zaleski
TRANSFORMATIONS
Awakening to the Sacred in Ourselves
An exploration of enlightenment experiences and
the ways in which they can transform our lives.
0-517-70150-2 Hardcover

David A. Cooper
ENTERING THE SACRED MOUNTAIN
Exploring the Mystical Practices of Judaism, Buddhism, and Sufism
An inspiring chronicle of one man's search for truth.
0-517-88464-X Softcover

215

Marc David
NOURISHING WISDOM
A Mind/Body Approach to Nutrition and Well-Being
A book that advocates awareness in eating.
0-517-88129-2 Softcover

Kat Duff
THE ALCHEMY OF ILLNESS
A luminous inquiry into the function and purpose of illness.
0-517-88097-0 Softcover

Joan Furman, MSN, RN, and David McNabb
THE DYING TIME
Practical Wisdom for the Dying and Their Caregivers
A comprehensive guide, filled with physical, emotional,
and spiritual advice.
0-609-80003-5 Softcover

Bernard Glassman
BEARING WITNESS
A Zen Master's Lessons in Making Peace
How Glassman started the Zen Peacemaker Order and
what each of us can do to make peace in our hearts and in the world.
0-609-60061-3 Hardcover

Bernard Glassman and Rick Fields
INSTRUCTIONS TO THE COOK
A Zen Master's Lessons in Living a Life That Matters
A distillation of Zen wisdom that can be used equally well as a manual on
business or spiritual practice, cooking or life.
0-517-88829-7 Softcover

Burghild Nina Holzer
A WALK BETWEEN HEAVEN AND EARTH
A Personal Journal on Writing and the Creative Process
How keeping a journal focuses and expands our awareness
of ourselves and everything that touches our lives.
0-517-88096-2 Softcover

Greg Johanson and Ron Kurtz
GRACE UNFOLDING
Psychotherapy in the Spirit of the Tao-te ching
The interaction of client and therapist illuminated
through the gentle power and wisdom of Lao Tsu's ancient classic.
0-517-88130-6 Softcover

Selected by Marcia and Jack Kelly
ONE HUNDRED GRACES
Mealtime Blessings
A collection of graces from many traditions, inscribed
in calligraphy reminiscent of the manuscripts of medieval Europe.
0-517-58567-7 Hardcover
0-609-80093-0 Softcover

Jack and Marcia Kelly
SANCTUARIES
A Guide to Lodgings in Monasteries, Abbeys, and Retreats
of the United States
For those in search of renewal and a little peace;
described by the *New York Times* as "the *Michelin Guide* of the retreat set."
THE NORTHEAST *0-517-57727-5 Softcover*
THE WEST COAST & SOUTHWEST *0-517-88007-5 Softcover*
THE COMPLETE U.S. *0-517-88517-4 Softcover*

Marcia and Jack Kelly
THE WHOLE HEAVEN CATALOG
A Resource Guide to Products, Services, Arts, Crafts, and Festivals
of Religious, Spiritual, and Cooperative Communities
All the things that monks and nuns do to support their habits!
0-609-80120-1 Softcover

Marcia M. Kelly
HEAVENLY FEASTS
Memorable Meals from Monasteries, Abbeys, and Retreats
Thirty-nine celestial menus from the more than 250 monasteries
the Kellys have visited on their travels.
0-517-88522-0 Softcover

Barbara Lachman
THE JOURNAL OF HILDEGARD OF BINGEN
A year in the life of the twelfth-century German saint—
the diary she never had the time to write herself.
0-517-59169-3 *Hardcover*
0-517-88390-2 *Softcover*

Katharine Le Mée
CHANT
The Origins, Form, Practice, and Healing Power of Gregorian Chant
The ways in which this ancient liturgy can nourish us
and transform our lives.
0-517-70037-9 *Hardcover*

Stephen Levine
A YEAR TO LIVE
How to Live This Year as if It Were Your Last
Using the consciousness of our mortality
to enter into a new and vibrant relationship with life.
0-609-80194-5 *Softcover*

Gunilla Norris
BEING HOME
A Book of Meditations
An exquisite modern book of hours,
a celebration of mindfulness in everyday activities.
0-517-58159-0 *Hardcover*

Ram Dass and Mirabai Bush
COMPASSION IN ACTION
Setting Out on the Path of Service
Heartfelt encouragement and advice for those ready
to commit time and energy to relieving suffering in the world.
0-517-88500-X *Softcover*

Rabbi Rami M. Shapiro
MINYAN
Ten Principles for Living a Life of Integrity
A primer for those interested to know
what Judaism has to offer the spiritually hungry.
0-609-80055-8 *Softcover*

Rabbi Rami M. Shapiro
WISDOM OF THE JEWISH SAGES
A Modern Reading of Pirke Avot
A third-century treasury of maxims on justice, integrity, and virtue—
Judaism's principal ethical scripture.
0-517-79966-9 Hardcover

Joan Tollifson
BARE-BONES MEDITATION
Waking Up from the Story of My Life
An unvarnished, exhilarating account of one woman's struggle
to make sense of her life.
0-517-88792-4 Softcover

Justine Willis Toms and Michael Toms
TRUE WORK
The Sacred Dimension of Earning a Living
Wisdom for the workplace from the husband-and-wife team
of NPR's weekly radio program *New Dimensions.*
0-517-70587-7 Hardcover

Ed. Richard Whelan
SELF-RELIANCE
*The Wisdom of Ralph Waldo Emerson
as Inspiration for Daily Living*
A distillation of Emerson's spiritual writings for contemporary readers.
0-517-58512-X Softcover

*Bell Tower books are for sale at your local bookstore
or you may call Random House at 1-800-793-BOOK to order with a credit card.*